FROM
Pillar
TO
Post

The Pearly Pellard Story

PEARL BROTHERTON

Pen Press Publishers Ltd
London

Published in the Great Britain by
Pen Press Publishers Ltd
39-41 North Road
Islington
London N7 9DP

ISBN 1 900796 33 3

A catalogue record of this book is available from the
British Library

Typesetting by Corrine Sherlock

DEDICATION

This book is dedicated to children everywhere who have had their civil liberties taken from them through mental or physical abuse. Children who have been humiliated beyond endurance and had the laughter taken from their young lives, and all caused by adults who should have known better.

To my two friends Pam Dawkins neé Clarbour, and Sheila Davey neé Fritche, for their friendship and support when I needed it most.

To my present husband Bryon and beloved sons, Andrew and Bryon, for any pain or humiliation that this book may cause them.

PREFACE

This is a bitter sweet account of the author's childhood during the years 1939 to 1956, and is set in various institutions throughout England. It represents the fear and humiliation that is felt by a child when abused, in any form, by an adult, and portrays how a child tries to overcome all of the obstacles. How ill-treatment can effect future relationships.

The names of some institutions and characters have been changed to protect any living relatives of those involved in this story.

ABOUT THE AUTHOR

Pearl Brotherton lives in a picturesque Leicestershire village with her husband and family. Despite her childhood experiences, by hard work and determination she has forged a successful career in accountancy. Recent media attention on child abuse in institutions prompted her to publish her own story.

CHAPTER ONE

My mind is in total confusion as I walk through the corridors of the small rural hospital to make my last visit to my dying mother, Eva. A mother whom I had never had the opportunity to know or love. Do I feel pity, compassion or resentment? I do not know. Bewilderment engulfs me as I inch my way towards the foot of the bed where she lays, her face ashen and drawn. A dreadful cancer is ravishing her slight body. She has suffered so much in life, and now this final blow.

She has a head of thick grey curly hair and even at this advanced stage in her illness, it looks magnificent. The nursing staff constantly admire its shine and texture. It makes no sense to me that I should be studying her hair at such a grave time.

Her breathing becomes more shallow and laboured. I speak, she murmurs on hearing my voice, yet I cannot take the few final paces between the foot of her bed and her side to comfort her, to put my arms around her, or hold her hand to ease her fears, to help her with her final journey. The embarrassment is far too great for me to do these things.

Tears stream down my cheeks as I close my eyes to shut out the infernal guilt that I am now feeling. These tears should be borne out of compassion and love at the thought of losing my mother, but they are not.

The memories of my hideous childhood cascade through my being like a thunderous waterfall flooding my mind. Memories that have been safely locked away were returning with fast abandon. Nothing could stop these nightmare images. Why were they haunting me at a time like this?

As dawn breaks, my mother takes her last breath. She lies still and lifeless and looks at peace. Yet no physical contact had taken place between us. Seeing my distressed state, Bryon my husband, took control of the situation. However, he did not know my story so could not understand the true identity of my distress. It was a story that I had locked away in a dark corner of my mind, where I had assumed, quite wrongly, that it would always stay.

I gather up my mother's few belongings and deposit them in the waste bin outside the hospital, just as if I am trying to rid myself of the past. This is easier said than done for my emotions are running high, and my renewed memories, now awoken, need to be explored.

CHAPTER TWO

I was born on the 19th July, 1939, the daughter of a coal miner, John Roberts, and his wife, a publican's daughter called Eva. They already had a son aged three years old named Peter John.

When I was born my head was covered in golden, curly hair; my granny mentioned that I resembled a little angel, therefore my mother decided to give me the name of Angela Jane. My father was asked to go to the City Registrar's Office to register my birth. On the way into the city he was waylaid by his drinking pals and ended up at the local pub, which was not at all unusual, ale houses were his way of life. Nothing was as important to him as his nightly tipple. He became so drunk that by the time he teetered into the Registrar's office, he had forgotten my name and registered me as Pearl June, probably the name of one of his many floozies. My mother and grandparents were most upset at his choice, however, my grandfather, making the best of a bad job, promptly nicknamed me "Pearly Pellard'.

On the day that I was being baptised, 3rd September, 1939, Britain declared war on Germany. Subsequently, my father was conscripted to fight for his country, which left us alone with our mother. My grandfather secured a property for the three of us, which was a three up and three down terraced house in the Aylestone Park district of Leicester.

The house was rented at a very low rent from the local plumber, on the condition that he was allowed to store his plumbing rubble in the back-yard. Cisterns, sinks and old toilet bowls were piled high giving an unsightly appearance to the property. The stench from them could be most obnoxious in the warm weather. Although out of bounds to us children, Peter and his pals turned the yard into their adventure playground, this was amongst my first recollections, because my mother despaired of me trying to copy the boys, resulting in my pretty dresses getting soiled and torn.

My mother had somewhat of a fetish about cleanliness. She would spend all day scrubbing and polishing the house over and over again. Whilst other children remember the smells of flowers and cooking, I remember the smell of bleach and lavender furniture polish. The small kitchen housed a red brick copper that was fired by coals beneath the cauldron, this was our only source of hot water. The copper would steam away all day, boiling the linen until it glittered like the white of snow. The gloss painted brick kitchen walls literally dripped with condensation and would form puddles on the red quarry floor tiles. The hot water would then be recycled to service my mother's endless cleaning.

Each morning Mum would lift Peter and I into the large white pot kitchen sink and scrub us both until we almost shone. We would then be dressed in freshly laundered clothes. It was then off to the local infants school for Peter, and I, only being three years old, attended the nursery class.

4

Each lunchtime Mum would collect us both from the school to take us to the local community centre, where war time lunches could be purchased for just a few pence. The centre was always alive and buzzing with the latest news about the war. Seen through the eyes of a child it was an enjoyable affair. My favourite meal was stew and dumplings stewed in giant saucepans and served by the voluntary workers. This would be followed by treacle suet pudding, which had been wrapped in old rags and steamed to perfection. Barely had Peter and I gobbled down our last spoonful, when Mum would whisk us away back to our home, where we would once again be stripped, placed in the white pot sink and scrubbed, garbed in clean clothes, then back to school for Peter for the afternoon session. When school was over for the day, we would go through the whole ritual of being bathed again. We must have been the cleanest children in the whole of Aylestone Park.

In the evenings we were allowed to go out into the street to play. There was no fear of abduction in those days, the streets were safe for children of all ages. Also, there was very little transport on the roads so no fear of being run over by a vehicle. My cousin Patricia and several small friends would call around to play such games as hopscotch and marbles. The older children would play whip and top. We were extravagant with our energy, very noisy and boisterous. I'm sure the childless neighbours breathed a sigh of relief when it was our bedtime.

When we returned home the blackout curtains

would be drawn to hide any light from the impending enemy that may be lurking in the skies. Peter and I would again be washed then dressed in our night attire. Peter then fetched out the board games, usually Snakes and Ladders, Ludo and Tiddly Winks, and the three of us would while away an hour. Peter always won because he liked to cheat. Mum wound up the record player and played the war time songs, the fire was stoked up, the setting was a really cosy scene.

Our house boasted a spacious cellar, which ran under the whole of the downstairs area of the house. When darkness fell, the three of us would gather our pillows and blankets and descend the cellar steps. Mum set up makeshift beds on the newly scrubbed brick cellar floor. "Come on you two, snuggle up close to keep warm, it's going to be a long night." Peter and I were only too pleased to obey, we needed to feel the closeness of her body for the extra security. Footsteps could often be heard rattling across the grating at the front of the house, a facility for the coalman to empty his sacks through. This saved him walking through the house in his dirty boots, Mum would have had a fit.

The shadows of the full moon often cast their beams through the grating, creating mysterious and frightening shadows, in all kind of shapes and sizes across the cellar floor. Often I would place my small hands over my eyes and peer through the partly opened fingers, this made the images look even more distorted. The light from the moonbeams reflected on the shiny black coals, giving the impression of tiny golden eyes dancing around in the half light, which in reality were only the minerals set in the coal. It was still scary enough to make me recoil in fear, causing me to snuggle ever closer into my mother's breast for comfort and reassurance.

Mum, speaking in whispers, related stories about harmful people who were out to kill us. People who were watching our every move through the walls of our house. I thought the footsteps on the grating belonged to the ogres she spoke of, when in reality they were just the footsteps of factory workers rushing home through the blackout from their twilight shifts.

Mum also told us that there were wild animals roaming about in the living rooms above us, waiting to pounce if we left the cellar during the night time hours. Peter often worsened the situation by making blood curdling noises to represent the animals, often I would become petrified with fear.

When daybreak came, we would gather together our bedding and climb back up the cellar steps. I half expected the animals to still be there, but the living rooms always looked normal.

Switching on the radio to listen to the news, Mum busied herself by preparing breakfast for us all. Everything was so normal it was just as though we had spent a normal night like any other normal family. Little did Peter and I realise that our nights were most abnormal, and were all part of our mother's schizophrenic existence.

CHAPTER THREE

One morning, Mum dressed Peter and I in our Sunday best clothes. Mine consisted of a tartan kilt, white blouse, red tie and black patent shoes. "We are going to visit Granny and Grandpa today," she said. This was odd as we never visited on a school day. Nevertheless, we were excited. It was always an adventure to visit our grandparents. They owned a beer and provision shop just thirty minutes walk away from our house.

Grandpa was a tall well-groomed person, with kind smiling eyes. Granny was a person of large proportions, who studied everyone from her wheelchair, which she had to frequent most of the time. She had steely blue eyes which could penetrate your very being. It was almost as if she could read your mind. Granny was a clever person and the brains behind the business. Grandpa had been a police officer before he had bought the shop. A job that he had thoroughly enjoyed, but had given up to nurse Granny. On each visit Grandpa would allow me to sit on the counter in his shop. He would help me to weigh 'Dolly Mixtures' or 'Jelly Babies' into three cornered bags. Sometimes I was allowed to eat some, but not often, food was rationed because of the war. Each bag would hold one ounce of sweets that would cost a penny or penny halfpenny per bag. A government food coupon would have to be proffered along with the money. No coupon, no sweets.

Customers would shuffle into the shop, many in their bedroom slippers, carrying large pot jugs. Handing the jug over they would say, "Put a couple of pints in there Charlie." (Charlie being my grandpa's name). The jug would be filled with ale from decorated pump handles housed on the counter, which was made from polished mahogany that my Uncle Charles, grandpa's son had crafted. "Gee the gel a copper," some customers would say. This was local dialect for give the girl a penny. On a good day I could collect twelve pennies making a whole shilling, which I would save in a large pink porcelain pig located on Grandpa's parlour shelf. Eventually I hoped to buy some silver tap dancing shoes, to wear at my tap dancing classes at the local Community Centre.

I loved to dance and show off, because I was a very precocious little girl. Oh how I loved those visits to my grandparents!

However, when we arrived on this particular day, everything appeared very different. There was no hustle and bustle of customers. The shop was in complete darkness. The closed sign had been displayed on the shop door. Grandpa was peering through the window awaiting our arrival. He immediately opened the shop door and we were ushered directly into the living quarters which were situated at the rear of the shop.

Granny sat in her wheelchair dabbing her eyes with a large white handkerchief. Her eyes appeared swollen and red from crying. Stretching out her hand she beckoned my mother to her side. "I'm so sorry Eva there is no other way," she wept. "It will only be for a short time, we will soon have you well again. Peter and Pearl will be well looked after." What did this mean? Where was Mum going? We dared not ask. Granny always said, "Children should be seen and not heard," or, "Only speak when you are spoken to."

Lunch was a miserable and silent affair that day. All the adults wept and Grandpa paced the floor. As soon as lunch was over Grandpa ushered Mum upstairs. Granny sat Peter and I down and in a matter of fact tone explained that our mother was going away on a short holiday. "Children are not allowed at the hotel," she said. "A car will come to collect your mum shortly."

Soon there was a loud rapping on the shop door. There stood a man wearing a uniform and a peaked black cap. "Come for Eva Roberts," he stated. Mum, her thin body racked with tears, was led out to a large black car. She did not look back. Peter and I could not understand why she was weeping, surely people did not weep who were going away on holiday. We concluded that she was weeping because she could not take us with her on her journey. I can still picture that day and that scene, me leaning up against the shop window and calmly waving Mum goodbye.

Grandpa opened up the shop for his evening customers, whilst Peter and I played the card game snap with Granny. We laughed and joked and had a lovely time. We were to sleep at our grandparents that night. This was such fun, we had never done this before. Grandpa tucked Peter and I into a large cosy bed, this was such a treat, it had been so long since we had slept in a bed at all. We giggled and bounced, and soon wearing ourselves out, we fell into a peaceful sleep.

The following morning we bounded down the stairs, to find that Grandpa had laid the table with boiled eggs and soldiers. He did most of the cooking because Granny could not stand for long periods of time.

We ate with relish, eggs were scarce during the war years and were very rarely served for breakfast. When we had eaten Grandpa washed and clothed us. "Now I have something to tell you both," he said, "come sit on my knee." Struggling for words he proceeded, "Granny is too poorly to look after you. I have the shop to run to bring in the money and you are both too young to fend for yourselves." He hesitated, taking deep breaths he continued. "Both of you will be sent to a children's home, until your mum comes back from her holiday." Feeling that he needed to add more to substantiate the story he continued, "Your mother is not too well, she needs a rest, with the war and all."

I was only four years of age and did not understand what a children's home was, but Peter being seven was far wiser. "It's where lots of children live together and get beaten when they are naughty," he said. "But don't worry Pearly Pellard, I will always look after you."

Although Peter teased me unmercifully he had always been protective towards me and would often confront other children who had upset me. He was a tough little boy and the neighbourhood children did not like to mess with him. I sometimes suspected that Peter felt as though I needed more protection than other little girls.

Later that morning, my Uncle Charles, a builder of some renown, arrived at the shop in his large black car, to transport Peter and I to the children's home. Uncle took up our small ready packed suitcases, and ushered us to his car. I sat on the back seat clutching my teddy bear Alfie with one hand and firmly clutching Peter's hand with my other.

It was quite an adventure travelling in a motor car. I sat up very straight so that I could be seen through the window, I felt very important and hoped people who knew me would notice me.

All too soon we reached our destination. Uncle pulled up outside a large imposing house in a very narrow road. Peter read aloud from a highly polished brass plaque on the wall of the house; 'The Millstone Lane Reception Hostel'. We stood there in awe, gazing up at the heavy wooden door sporting a large polished brass knocker which Uncle knocked, rat a tat tat. The echo could be heard deep inside the building. We heard the sound of footsteps crossing a hard floor. Soon the door was opened by a lady of large proportions wearing a white overall.

"This must be Peter and Pearl Roberts! Do come in," she said. Uncle Charles declined the offer. He bent to kiss us both, handed us our small suitcases. Then with tears in his eyes he turned on his heel, got back into his car and drove away.

We entered a large hall, which, with its stone tiled floor appeared cold and uninviting. The reality of our situation suddenly hit us. We were alone, we had to stay in this place, the day's adventure was over. Peter began to scream and cry. "I don't want to stay in this place, let me go home." The lady in white held him down telling him to behave himself. He struggled, she slapped his face. I began to sob, neither of us had ever been smacked before.

We were whisked into a bathroom housing a large white bath that had running water coming from the taps. Peter and I had only been bathed in a sink or a tin bath in front of the fire, the idea of climbing into this huge contraption was awesome. "Come, take off all your clothes the pair of you," we were ordered. Peter declined and said he was not stripping off in front of anyone, he felt he was far too old to bare himself to strangers. Within seconds we were both forcibly stripped and tossed roughly into the bath. We were both screaming so much that I'm sure we nearly brought the house down.

Still struggling we were covered in a foul smelling solution and scrubbed until our little bodies were bright red. When we were dressed we were led into another room where a slight lady sat behind a desk.

"I'm the Matron," she said. "Welcome to Millstone Lane. You will be well looked after, receive fine meals, and taught your lessons, but we will not tolerate bad behaviour or tantrums, the like of which you have just subjected my staff to. If your mother was prepared to put up with such tantrums that was up to her, but here

13

you will behave." She droned on and on about house rules, but Peter and I were far too young to understand much about her lecture at all. There was no leeway given to the fact that this was the first time that we had been away from home or indeed away from our mother.

At bedtime I was taken to a dormitory, which I was to share with several other girls. I had my beloved teddy Alfie with me. That night I kept getting out of my bed and walking the landings looking for Peter. Eventually I received a good smacked bottom for my troubles. I pulled the sheets over my head and cried myself to sleep.

One morning a few days later, Peter ushered me into the broom cupboard. "Keep quiet Pearly Pellard. I am going to take you away from here, but it is our secret." We crept out of the back door and down through the garden. He lifted me onto the wall then climbed over and lifted me down. We ran and ran until we reached the Victoria Park, where we spent most of the day playing. The day wore on and I got extremely tired and hungry. We had no money to buy food. "Please take me back," I pleaded. By now I had begun to sob. "Peter I've the tummy ache I'm so hungry." Being only seven Peter was in a bit of a dilemma, and he then decided to take me to Grandpa's.

The walk seemed miles to my small legs, in fact Grandpa's was only two miles away and within the hour we were back at the beer shop. Grandpa looked absolutely stunned to see us. He found it remarkable that Peter had found his way and suggested that he was like a homing pigeon. "We've run away," blurted

Peter. "We didn't like their bread and butter at the home. We want to come here and stay with you," Peter said crying. "Please, please," he begged. Grandpa told him that this was not possible.

Grandpa put on his coat and went out for a while. He returned with a policeman, who in a stern voice boomed "Now what's this then running away from the home and causing your Grandparents so much upset." I was really scared and hid behind Peter for protection. In a small voice I pipe up "I've come back for my money out of my pot pig to buy my silver dancing shoes." Somehow I felt the need to take the blame for running away, it must have been a child's instinct to protect Peter. Although my attempts were fruitless because a decision was made to separate Peter and I. "A bad influence on me," he was told. I ended up back at Millstone Lane and Peter was sent elsewhere.

Strange as it may seem, I soon fitted into the regimented way of the home. There were no hugs or cuddles from the staff, we were treated in a very clinical way. We were given orders and we were expected to obey. I became a rebellious little girl, often throwing tantrums. Matron would grab my golden curls and slap my face. The more slaps I received, the more rebellious I became.

Then one morning the maid summoned me into Matron's office. There sat my Uncle Charles, I ran to him and hugged him not ever wanting to let him go. "Would you like to come home with me Pearly Pellard?" he asked. I shrieked with delight. "Oh yes please, can we go now!" My case was fetched from the stores,

Alfie my teddy bear was returned to me, and after a few goodbyes we were on our way. "Will Peter and Mum be coming to stay with you too?" I asked on our homeward journey. Uncle said that wouldn't be possible but gave no further explanation on the matter.

I did not know at the time that my mother was never coming home from her holiday. She was not at a hotel but was in the 'City Lunatic Asylum', and had been certified as being insane. There was great stigma attached to this type of illness in 1943.

CHAPTER FOUR

U ncle drove out into the countryside, eventually arriving at a large semi detached house, in a village named Groby. We drove up a large drive, to be welcomed by my Auntie Nellie and my two cousins, Charlie and Eric. Charlie was a sturdy boy aged ten who had a happy smiling face and Eric was a shy, studious boy of seven. The boys chased to the back of the car to collect my few belongings from the boot, whilst Aunt Nellie ushered me inside. "Welcome to your new home Pearl," she said. "Be a good girl and we shall get along fine."

The three of us went into the large garden to explore. "Oh, chickens!" I shrieked, as I spotted the hen house at the bottom of the garden. I ran amongst them, they clucked and flapped their wings in total annoyance. "You mustn't do that, the hens will stop laying if you frighten them," said Charlie.

Later, my Aunt introduced me to my new bedroom which had been decorated in pink. The small bed was covered with a pink eiderdown embroidered with white ducks. There was a wardrobe in which hung three flowered dresses draped on satin coat hangers smelling of lavender. I placed my teddy Alfie on the pillow. I just could not wait to get into bed. I had my wash in a proper bathroom and chased across the landing stark naked much to the astonishment of my two cousins. Snuggling down under the clean sheets, I at last felt happy and contented.

It was decided that I would be sent to a private school in the City, a school called 'Clark's College'. On my first morning I was dressed in a smart maroon coloured uniform, which we had bought in the City a few days previously. I must have spent nearly half an hour preening myself in front of the mirror. Auntie Nellie told me what a lucky girl I was to receive such a fine education, pointing out that I must be very well behaved.

A very spiteful boy sat at the back of me in the classroom, he found great pleasure in pulling my curly hair. This made me so angry, I would turn and pinch him, but this did not seem to deter him any. Sunk into the end of my desk was a small inkwell, filled with blue ink. One day I became so angry with this boy that I just picked up this inkwell, turned and threw the blue liquid all over him. After only three months at the school the Principal expelled me. Uncle Charles tried to be reasonable about the incident and implied that I had inherited my mother's hot temper. From then on I attended the local village school. I settled down a lot better there and could soon read and write very well, and being a very outgoing child I liked to stand up and read to the rest of the class.

Charlie, Eric and I had many happy times roaming the nearby countryside. Searching for birds' nests, fishing in streams or we would just play childhood games such as tic and hide and seek in the garden.

Winter came, and we went to the Groby Pool to play on the ice, we would slide and skate. One morning when we arrived, the ice was getting very thin in places, the thaw had begun. Charlie warned "Keep off the ice Pearl," but no I always thought I knew best. After several steps onto the ice, the ice cracked and I could feel myself sinking into the murky freezing water. Charlie managed to pull me out, at great danger to himself. He took me home and changed me into dry clothes. He was so loyal he never did tell his mum.

I soon had a special bond with my Uncle Charles. When he came in from work, I would climb onto his knee, before either of the boys had the chance to do so, I expected him to be very selfish with his affections and save them all for me. Like most war time babies I was unused to a father figure in my life, and Uncle Charles was not used to girl children, and was quite taken back with my floods of affection towards him.

After staying with my Uncle for a year, the war came to an end. Everyone was so joyful, we had endless parties and celebrated by burning an effigy of 'Hitler' on the 'Groby Road Island', a large island set in the middle of the road. Shortly after the end of the war my Uncle sat me down and gently explained that because the war had ended, it was time for me to return to my father, as it was now my father's responsibility to take care of me. Also, Auntie Nellie was pregnant and did not feel that she could carry the added burden of a new baby and myself. It was a shame because I was so looking forward to nursing the new baby. I had also come to think of Charles and Eric as my brothers, even telling everyone at school that they were. But any pleas to stay were in vain, the decision had been made for me to depart.

The year that I had spent with my Uncle was so happy, and for that year I was to be eternally grateful, for the following years were not to be as idyllic. The following morning Uncle drove me back to my father, to the house where I had been born. Any recollection of the house had long been forgotten, so it was somewhat of a shock to draw up outside a dingy dwelling. There was no love lost between my Uncle and my father, my parents had been forced to marry because my mother had been pregnant with my brother Peter. A situation greatly frowned upon in 1936. The two adults just glared at each other and my Uncle handed me over, instructed my father to take care of me, then kissed me goodbye and left, leaving me once again with a heavy heart.

There were no hugs or kisses from my father considering that he had not seen me since shortly after my birth. The loneliness which I had experienced when I had been parted from Peter returned as I entered the house. My nostrils filled with a nauseous smell of tobacco and stale ale. The house felt damp and cold, no coal fire burned in the grate. My father turned to me, saying, "I don't know why Charlie's brought you back here, I can't look after you, I've made arrangements to take you to Bagworth tomorrow to your Uncle Cecil's." I had no idea who Uncle Cecil was, and had never heard of Bagworth.

For most of the afternoon I sat in the chair sulking and crying, desperately wanting to go back to Uncle Charlie's and play with my cousins. A wish I knew would not be granted.

There was very little food in the house, so my father fetched me a bag of chips from the 'Chippie' opposite the house, sliced me a chunk of stale bread, then I sat and ate them out of newspaper.

"Got to go out now Pearly, don't answer the door to anyone," my father informed me. He put on his coat and went out. There I sat, a six year old child with no heating in the middle of winter all alone. I felt petrified.

After what seemed like hours my father returned, swaying as he walked, breath reeking with the smell of ale. "Here you are lass, I have brought you a peach for being a good girl." Feeling both hungry and excited, for I'd never seen a peach before, I snatched it from his hands. The peach turned out to be an apple, but my father was too drunk to know the difference.

That night I slept in an armchair with a blanket around me, the spare beds in the house were damp, they had not been used since my mother had been taken away, but Dad still went upstairs to bed. His snoring could be heard all over the house.

The following day was Saturday. We set off on a long bus journey to Bagworth. Bagworth turned out to be a small mining village some twelve miles from the city. The streets were heavy with coal dust, though once out of the village centre there were open fields. We walked for quite some time down country lanes until we reached a dairy, which was owned by my uncle Cecil and Auntie Elsie. It was not a self producing dairy just one that sold milk. This was to be my new home. There were two other children much older than myself in the family, a boy named Tony and a girl Freda.

The house was small but cosy, a large coal fire roared in the grate giving a homely atmosphere. I was to share a double bed with Freda my cousin, she could not come to terms with the fact that I was so young and used to force me to smoke cigarettes which made me feel quite poorly. One day, her mother found out and she soon put a stop to it.

My Uncle and Aunt were good to me, but did not show me the same affection as Uncle Charles and Auntie Nellie had done. My Grandma Roberts lived in the same village, down a long dirt path that led to nowhere, with the exception of her wooden bungalow. She reared pigs and poultry, which she killed and cured herself. Often I would sit in her kitchen whilst she pulled the neck of a hen, it would then run around and around with its head hanging limply to one side. She would take me to the railway sidings to collect slack to stoke her fire. Always she would say to me, "Your father's a bad 'un Pearl, he should be looking after you, not hanging around public bars. The war has changed him a lot, he was taken prisoner, and has not been the same since."

Barely had I settled in, when my Auntie Elsie told me that she was returning me to my father. Apparently my Aunt had only taken me in, for financial consideration. My father had not kept to his end of the bargain, and had not come up with the money for my keep. Times were hard, being so soon after the war, they could not afford to keep me for nothing.

I was put on a bus and my father met me at the bus

station at my destination. Upon arrival he informed me that he was taking me to a children's home that day, that it had already been arranged.

CHAPTER FIVE

My father and I arrived at the 'Counteshorpe Cottage Homes'. It was a beautiful summer's day in late June, three weeks before my seventh birthday. The Homes looked idyllic. They consisted of eleven large Victorian houses, set out in a semi-circle on a gravelled road, known as 'The Drive'. The houses were fronted by a large field, with swings, slides and sand pits dotted around. There was a small farm at the rear end of the field, where some cows were grazing peacefully. At the rear of 'The Cottages' lay vegetable gardens, set with neatly lined cabbages, carrots, and lettuces. There was a nursery for the under fives, a small isolation hospital and a laundry.

On ringing the bell at the gate, a spotty faced teenage boy appeared, demanding to know what our business was. "Admitting Pearl Roberts," my father replied. The spotty faced boy admitted us, then led us down the drive to 'The Main Reception'. This was a beautiful looking building with a brightly polished knocker and letterbox on a freshly painted door, which stood open giving full view of a majestic hall. The building was known as 'The Residence.' This was where the Superintendent and his wife lived. They looked like country gentry, she in her tweed suit and brogues, him in his plus fours.

My father signed numerous forms which gave my guardianship to The Cottage Homes. It was then explained that each of the cottages housed between twelve and twenty children. Some designated for boys and some for girls, but never mixed. Each cottage had a number and name. I was designated to number eleven, The Gables. Some cottages were run by House Mothers and Fathers, and some by just House Mothers.

After my father had carried out his business, he left looking extremely relieved that he had discharged his duties as a father. It was almost impossible to put my feelings of desolation into words. To be dumped by one's father, simply because he preferred the pub to his own daughter, was totally bewildering for one so young.

The Superintendent, 'Super' as he was known by the children, delivered me to 'The Gables', where I met my House Mother, Miss Mather. She was a middle aged spinster. Tall, and dressed in elegant black clothes. I stared at her hair in fascination. She wore her hair in plaits that were wound around and around her head, which reminded me of telephone headsets stuck to the side of her head. Her teeth were prominent and prevented her from closing her mouth properly. When she spoke I thought that she had got a plum stuck in her mouth, she spoke in such a la de da way.

"So this is Pearl Roberts," Miss Mather said. "I have been expecting you. What a dirty child you look, you must be bathed instantly." I was soon to learn that she suffered from the same obsession of cleanliness as my mother.

After my bath I was sprayed with DDT and my

hair was drenched in a foul smelling substance, "just in case of fleas," Miss Mather said. Miss Mather told me that I was to call her 'Ma'. I was issued with a uniform, emblazoned across each item was written 'The Cottage Homes, 11PJR'. The number of my cottage and the initials of my name. I felt as though I had been branded.

It was now time for lunch. There were fourteen girls of varying ages sitting at the tables in the dining room, each one was dressed in identical clothes. They all turned to stare at me as 'Ma' introduced me as Pearl Roberts, another poor unfortunate that no one wanted. Ma pointed at one of the older girls and said, "Betty you will look after Roberts, show her the ropes and make sure she toes the line." This was my first introduction to life in The Cottage Homes.

Bedtime came and Betty took me to the dormitory that was situated in the attic. The ceiling which was high, formed an apex, that exposed rafters creating a cold and foreboding atmosphere. The only natural light came from a very small window on the gable end and a fan light set in the roof. The floor boards were uncovered, they were painted with a dark coloured varnish, each girl took it in turns to polish these with a large heavy buffer, the end result had to be perfection. "Put some elbow grease into it," Ma would scold as we sweated away with aching backs, age was no barrier to this chore.

There were seven iron-framed beds set out on either side of the room, each covered in a white cotton eiderdown. There was a small locker standing at the side of each bed, in which we kept all our worldly goods, including our spare set of clothes. My issue was laid out on the bed, my new wardrobe consisted of two vests, two rubber buttoned liberty bodices, two flannelette petticoats, two jumpers and two skirts and two pairs of navy blue bloomers.

My cottage and number were also emblazoned on all of these. We were expected to change the whole of our clothes just once a week. Not very hygienic, but this was classed as being ultra clean in those days.

I was renowned for my vivid imagination, and once lights were out I could see all manner of ghostly shadows set in the rafters. I must have fallen into a fitful sleep; I awoke with my cheeks covered in tears. Betty had her hand over my mouth. "Shut up you noisy little brat, you have been screaming and have woken us all. For this you must pay," said Betty. She stripped off my nightdress, and as I stood stark naked she lifted me up until I could touch the rafters. "Clasp hold of the rafters Roberts," Betty bade. "Now just hang there until you can stop being such a whimp." I must have hung there for at least twenty minutes, my hands and arms were numb with the strain, not to mention the cold. Each time I disobeyed Betty after that I received the same punishment.

Each morning we would rise at five forty-five, wash, dress in overalls, breakfast and then carry out chores, which consisted of scrubbing, polishing, cleaning windows and peeling vegetables for the evening meal. We would then change into our school uniform and assemble on the drive outside The Residence. School

27

buses would arrive and take us to various schools spread throughout the city. I was to attend Hazel Street School. Standing on The Drive on my first school morning, a boy in spectacles approached me. "Well if it's not Pearly Pellard!" he exclaimed.

"How do you know my nickname?" I retorted not recognising this boy.

"I'm your brother Peter," he declared. He was living in cottage five. I had not recognised him because of his spectacles and a bad squint in his eye, apparently caused by a bad dose of measles. After this first emotional meeting we arranged to meet every morning at the school bus. It was wonderful to find my brother again after such a long time. Although not housed in the same cottage, I felt safer knowing that he was around. Although our relationship was never constant, because each time he committed a petty crime he got shipped off for short spells in remand homes to teach him a lesson.

My first day at school was quite a memorable one. During morning assembly the Headmaster announced that he wished all children from the Cottage Homes to stay behind when assembly had finished. The other children filed out sneering at us as they went. "Right," said the Headmaster. "A sum of money has been stolen from the cloakroom. Which one of you has taken it?" No one owned up so we were all searched. Why me I do not know being my first day at school. Apparently this was the norm, whatever misdemeanour occurred at the school, the children from the Cottage Homes were always blamed. Often, when I was naughty in the classroom, my form teacher would shout sarcastically, "Please behave yourself 11PJB," referring to the labels on my clothes. My so-called class mates soon followed suit and I was nicknamed '11PJ'. I despised and detested this school and learnt very little during my time there. My behaviour became appalling, I quite fancied myself as the class comic. Most of my time was spent in the corridor outside the classroom door with my hands placed on my head.

When the school wrote to 'Ma' about my behaviour, she almost had a seizure, she ranted and raved, pulled my hair, threw me onto the floor and kicked me unmerifully. "One of my girls showing me up in this manner, I will not tolerate it. Do you hear me girl?" she ranted. Not only had I heard, I had felt. Still not satisfied, Ma sent me to 'The Residence', for further punishment. This was to be by the way of 'The Flogger', a leather strap with thongs attached. After six strokes administered by 'Super' I was very sore, but unrepentant. That flogging was to be the first of many for me. As 'Ma' would say, "Your tongue runs away with itself, and will always keep you in trouble."

Life at The Gables was never very easy. Ma had no compassion for any of the girls. She would fly into rages at the slightest provocation, always lashing out with her fists or feet or any other instrument that may be handy whilst in a rage, the girl at the nearest range would always 'cop for it'.

Ma's private sitting room was adorned with expensive carpets, furniture and ornaments. It was a frightening experience to have to clean the room, in case we dropped or broke anything. We girls would take it in turns to serve her meals on delicate china, she always ate alone in her room. One day, my turn came to serve her a meal. I entered the room with the meal set out on a silver tray lined with a delicate lace tray cloth. We were made to curtsey on entry into her room, which often proved rather difficult given that we were carrying a tray laden with food. As I curtsied, a drop of gravy from the gravy boat dripped onto her beautifully polished table, which us girls had spent many hours accomplishing. Ma was out of her chair in a flash, like a woman demented she kicked the tray out of my hand, the contents splattering around the room creating a frightful mess. She pummelled me with her fists so much, I thought I was going to pass out. Screaming at the top of her voice Ma called for Betty. "Why haven't you trained this brat properly?" and immediately slapped Betty around the face. "The pair of you can forfeit your meal, and clean up this mess you have caused." We were cleaning for hours. Still bruised and sore from my afternoon's encounter, come bedtime, Betty gave me the rafter treatment. Betty didn't take any prisoners and whatever caused the present predicament just didn't count. Poor Betty was just fed up to the back teeth of paying for my mistakes.

One Friday night Betty had a bad dream and wet the bed. Shaking me awake she quickly changed all of her bed linen, including the mattress, for my dry ones. I lay there for the rest of the night in her urine. On learning that my bed was wet Ma decided to punish me. I was made to stand in the outside toilet, wearing nothing but the urinated sheet for the whole of Saturday. The following night I was to spend the whole night in the coal shed in just my night attire. "See if you can wet yourself in there," Ma retorted. In the pitch of night owls hooted and each sound made me tremble. I was petrified but had to see the punishment through, we girls just did not welsh on each other.

The food we were served at The Cottage Homes was often grim. The worst being a watery stew with lumps of yellow fat floating on the surface. If the food wasn't eaten at dinner time, it would be served for breakfast the next day, and each subsequent meal until it had been eaten. Often I would hold the fat in my mouth until I could find an appropriate time to spit it out. When questioning children from some of the other cottages they seemed to enjoy a slightly better diet than us. This was because Miss Mather used to distribute the rations amongst her elite friends when they came to visit. We wrapped eggs and cheese into parcels tying them neatly for her friends to take away with them.

One morning I awoke to find that a scab had grown on my face. "What an ugly filthy sight you look Roberts," Ma screeched as I entered the kitchen for my early morning chores. "Only filthy girls get things like that, those who don't wash get scabs. Get out of my kitchen, you will contaminate it. I must punish you." I was put on outside toilet duties for a week, for something that nature had created. Each time she saw me she prodded me or pulled my hair and made snide remarks about the scab.

One night as I lay in bed, I thought, 'I'll pick the scab off, then Ma will leave me alone.' The deed done, I began to panic. What should I do with the scab? If Ma found it in the dormitory I would get another beating. So, without further ado I ate it. The following day was a Saturday, now I would get a reprieve from Ma's bickering and prodding. But how wrong can one be. As soon as I entered the dining room, Ma zoomed in on me like a vulture after it's prey. "Ah Roberts, I see your scab has disappeared, where is it?

Lost for words I stammered, "Um ha, I've thrown the scab out of the bedroom window Ma."

"You filthy beast," she screeched, "Contaminating my nice garden with your filth." She clapped her hands, the dining room fell silent. "All of you will search for Robert's scab in the garden after breakfast. No further meals will be served until you have found it." Each girl turned and glared at me. Saturday was the only day on which we were given any free time, to play on the field and chat to other residents from the other cottages. We searched for what seemed hours, the girls were making nasty remarks and threats. Come lunchtime my tummy was rumbling with hunger, we had missed morning cocoa and now we were about to miss out on lunch too. I decided it was time to confess to Ma. "Please Ma," I hesitated, "I didn't throw the scab out of the window, I ate it." The palm of her hand hit me with such force it knocked me off balance. I sported a black eye for weeks. And I still had to face the wrath of the other girls later.

There were also good times in the Cottages. On

Sunday mornings we would dress up in our best clothes. In the summer it consisted of a blue Gingham dress, navy blazer, and straw Panama hat. These could be seen hanging in a row in a special room. It almost looked like a school uniform shop.

All the children from each cottage would congregate in The Drive, then walk through the village crocodile style to the Countesthorpe Parish Church. The villagers would often step out of their houses to watch us pass, and offer a friendly word.

We all but filled the church. I liked to sing the hymns, but soon got fidgety when the parson gave his sermon from the pulpit. I would study the stained glass windows and make stories up in my mind about the pictures. Ma said that God would send me to hell for not listening.

On Guy Fawkes night we had a huge bonfire, with lots of fireworks donated by various charities. Local dignitaries attended. We had sausages, hot potatoes and roasted chestnuts. The older children took days to make a life-like guy. The night air would be filled with the rendering of the children's voices singing camp fire songs. Lady Barnet, a patron for the charity of the Homes, would come along to ignite the fire. At the first flame, cries of 'hip, hip hurrah' could be heard for miles.

At Christmas time, a huge Christmas tree, with lights and baubles would be erected on the field, outside The Residence. On Christmas Eve all of the children would hold lighted candles, whilst singing carols around the tree. On Christmas morning we would all receive a very small gift from the Board of Governors. The gifts would normally have been donated by various local charities. Some children had gifts from relatives. One year I was lucky, a parcel was delivered to me wrapped in brown paper, addressed to P.J. Roberts. Excitedly I tore off the paper to find a jigsaw puzzle and a tin of chocolates. Half of the chocolates were scoffed in minutes. Sometime later there was a knock at the tradesman's entrance door. "Roberts," Ma called, " Your brother Peter is here." In his hand he held a parcel wrapped in brown paper.

"Got this parcel this morning Pearly, it must have been meant for you because it's a doll, and a tin of chocolates." Both of our initials were P.J. and there had clearly been a mix-up. I gave Peter his jigsaw puzzle and the chocolate that was left. Poor Peter ended up with half rations. My father never sent me any Christmas gifts, and neither did he visit.

One Christmas, the Leicester Chronicle carried an article about the Homes, the idea was to try to persuade local folk to take a child into their home for Christmas. Because I never received any visitors at any time, the Home hoped that I would be one of the chosen ones. I had my photograph taken and it was displayed alongside the article. I was lucky, someone obviously like the look of me and I was chosen.

Come Christmas Eve day it was all actions go. First a new 'bubble' style hair cut, and set. What a transformation from my normal unruly mop! Then off down to The Residence, where I was rigged from top to toe in new clothes. With my spare clothes packed in a suitcase, I was impatient to be away.

Around midday my 'Christmas Parents' arrived. Nervously eyeing them, I extended my hand for a polite handshake, as I had been instructed to do so by Ma. The gentleman was a tall quietly spoken man, his wife was profoundly deaf with severe speaking difficulties. They must have been about forty years of age. To say I was disappointed was an understatement. They were nothing like the image that I had conjured up in my romantic imagination, which was something along the lines of Royalty. I was instructed to call them Uncle and Aunt.

On the way to their home, Uncle explained that they did not have children of their own, but would very much like to adopt an older child like me. My hopes began to rise as I reassessed the situation. Cunningly I thought, if I'm on my best behaviour they might choose me. To get away from Ma would be heaven; no more beatings. I prayed really hard in church to get away from Ma, perhaps 'God' had heard me after all.

On arriving at their small but neat home, I was quickly made to feel like one of the family. A blazing coal fire burned in the hearth, a Christmas tree twinkling with lights stood in the corner, paper streamers stretched across the room. It was like a scene that I could only remember from Christmas cards. This was always what I had wanted, love, warmth, a cosy home and someone to shower attention on me. Neighbours kept popping in to welcome me, the 'Christmas Child' I was called. I loved it all, I was the centre of attention.

My 'Christmas Aunt' brushed my golden curls until they shone, and threaded a bright red ribbon into my hair. Then allowed me to admire myself in the mirror. My 'Christmas bedroom', was prettily decorated with chintz curtains and bed cover. Balloons hung from the ceiling and silver tinsel adorned the headboard. A table lamp with pretty shade stood on the bedside cabinet. It was a world apart from the stark attic dormitory which I was used to.

I awoke on Christmas morning, with the usual excitement of an eight year old. Piled at the side of the bed were mounds of toys. A doll, a doll's cot, books, jigsaws and skipping rope. Never had I been so fortunate. I whooped with joy. On hearing me, my 'Christmas Uncle' came to my room to share in the excitement, although it was barely daybreak. Wrapping paper covered the carpet but I didn't get a smack for being untidy. Instead he sat on the edge of the bed, and took me on his knee, hugging me and cuddling me. This left me with a warm glow so I snuggled up closer to him. Suddenly his hand began to stroke my legs, rubbing up and down, then on to my thighs and bottom, stroking away. Warning bells flashed through my mind. I knew what was happening could not be right, he was breathing heavily. My little body went rigid with fright, "Please Mister, don't do that," I pleaded. "Ma wouldn't like you doing that." He continued to stroke me so I bit his hand. He fled from the room. I spent the following two days sulking. My Christmas dream had been broken. On my return to number 11, Ma immediately called me to her sitting room. As soon as I entered she began to scream, "You ungrateful little bitch. You just could not behave yourself, biting that nice gentleman like that." He never wants to set eyes on you again." It was pointless trying to tell my side of the story, it would not have been believed. Shrugging my shoulders I walked away. I was so used to disappointments, that I was past caring.

CHAPTER SIX

Each summer the whole of The Cottage Homes would go away on a fortnight's holiday. The venue was always the same, the Mablethorpe Seaside Camp. Preparing to go was a mammoth task, with lots of hustle and bustle, squabbles, fighting and smacks. Once there, we would sleep in large marquees, set out in a field, just a short walk from the beach. The meals would be served from a hut, members of each cottage would take turns to prepare the food. Mostly, weather permitting, we would eat alfresco.

Famous stars would come to entertain us. One summer Margaret Lockwood came to visit us, and some of us were to have our photograph taken with her, but to my disappointment, I could not be included. I had recently had surgery for gangrene on my finger, which still had an unsightly bandage binding it, and the bandage was now filthy. "We cannot have you ruining the picture with that filthy bandage, Roberts," Ma declared. I sulked for much of the day, but consoled myself with the fact that Margaret Lockwood had spoken to me, enquiring after my finger, asking me what I had done to hurt it.

After chores we would go to the beach to play games and swim. In the evenings we would sit around the campfires and sing songs. I would always sing a solo song called *The Gypsy Queen*.

My renderings filled the night air. "The sun is setting

in the west, it's time for gypsies now to rest. Goodnight to all, said the Queen, and round the camp fire I will sit and dream." I would warble. 'Showing off', as Ma called it. One autumn we staged a concert at the Co-operative Hall, in Leicester. All funds raised went towards the upkeep of the Homes. When we went to the audition we all tried to outdo each other, the stakes were high. It wasn't just being in the show that mattered, it also meant spending three whole days away from the Home, and our normal chores.

I was now eight years of age and old enough to audition. I was chosen to sing and enact a song called *The Little Milk Maid*. Within days I had learnt my words and actions to perfection. I would practice all over the place whilst doing chores, even in the dormitory, much to the distaste of Betty who had not been chosen to do anything.

We performed at two matinees and three evening performances. Local drama groups and theatre companies loaned us the costumes. The auditorium was packed at each performance. Leicester was a city of theatre-goers in the forties and our show always offered something a little different. We were deprived kids trying to prove ourselves which we always managed to achieve on those occasions, and often the outcome would be hilarious.

On another occasion a real live cowboy came to perform at a city theatre. All the children from The Cottages were invited free of charge. Five children were chosen from the audience to go onto the stage and ride on a tin Triangle horse which moved by manoeuvring little bars on the side of the horse with our feet. The first across the stage won a prize. I was chosen to ride, but did not win. However, the cowboy still presented me with a large cocoa tin filled with round bars of chocolate. I treasured mine so much that I saved them too long causing the chocolate to go mouldy.

So you see, life was not all bad at The Cottage Homes. It was just unfortunate that the public only saw the good side, and was therefore, totally unaware of what went on in some cottages, especially The Gables.

Some months passed by, with the usual humdrum of life. Attending school, doing chores and still receiving my fair share of beatings. I was now approaching my ninth birthday and was becoming a right little tough nut. After a beating I would shout, "That didn't hurt," and would immediately receive another beating. I was either too stubborn or too stupid to keep my mouth shut. Life was tough; the only way to get through it was to act tough, otherwise it would have been easy to go under and lose oneself altogether. I had seen it happen with many girls, they had become snivelling wrecks.

It was the Whitsuntide holidays and we had a week's break from school. As usual, I was being punished for some misdemeanour by being made to work in the laundry. One particular day I was filling the large boiler with linen, when one of the younger residents from my cottage came running into the laundry. "Ma wants you back at the cottage now," said the girl gasping for breath for she had run so hard. "Your dad's here to see you."

"Don't lie!" I spat for I did not believe her, my dad had never once visited me in all the time that I had been in the Home. "If I find you're lying I'll beat your brains in," I told her venomously. Back at number eleven, I found that she had told me the truth. There stood my dad. I eyed him curiously. Many times I had spent day-dreaming about this day, when my dad would come to the Home and take me away. Often I had imagined how it would be. In my dreams Dad would drive up to the Home in a big white car, throw himself at my feet begging for my forgiveness for leaving me in this place. He'd tell me how much he loved me and that life was now going to be idyllic. I'd often lied to the other girls about my father telling them that he was an army officer who guarded important posts overseas, explaining that this was why I was in the Home, and that my Mother was a famous dancer in America and that one day they would both come and fetch me. Sometimes I think that I half believed the lies myself.

To my dismay, instead of telling me how much he loved me, he calmly stood there and said, "Hello Pearl, I've come to take you and Peter home. I can't afford the thirty bob a week that this place charges me for your keep." There was no hug, no kiss in fact no contact at all.

My belongings, which were few, were quickly gathered together and placed in brown paper carrier bags. Ma's parting words were, "You will have a job to control that one, she has a will of her own. You will wish you had paid your thirty shillings, when you have had her for a week." We left number eleven with farewells left unspoken, for my friends were working at their various chores. Much to my relief in some respects, otherwise they would have known that I had told them lies about my father.

We headed for The Residence, where Peter awaited. A doctor entered the room, he examined Peter and I before we were discharged to prove that we were in good physical condition, before being allowed to leave the Home. The Doctor did not mention the bruising on my body from the beatings I had received from Ma. He must have been used to seeing them on other children, and possibly thought that I had deserved them.

After the examination, my father signed some papers and the Superintendent discharged Peter and I. We were fast becoming names on a form.

We all walked to the bus stop. Dad made no attempt to hold our hands. Once on the bus he blurted out, "I've got you both a new mam, your own mam is dead. If you both behave yourselves, I'll keep you."

Peter and I looked at each other stunned, no one at the Home had informed us about the death of our mother, or allowed us to attend her funeral. Unlike my friend Evelyn, when her dad had died the Super had called her to The Residence and she'd been told properly, and her House Mother had taken her to the funeral.

Peter wanted to know how Mum had died, but Dad was very evasive, he just pretended to concentrate on the cigarette, which he was rolling in a paper with tobacco that he had taken from a gold coloured tin. He then took deep puffs from the cigarette and stared out of the bus window until we reached our destination. Although recollections of my mother were few, I suddenly felt like half of an orphan and tears slid down my face. Somehow it only seemed proper to cry. Dad seemed completely oblivious to my tears and offered no kind words of comfort. "Shut up Pearl," Peter said. "You can't even remember what Mum looked like." Dad began to look uncomfortable, it was obvious that he wasn't used to being around children, or able to cope with their fickle emotions.

CHAPTER SEVEN

We turned into Lorrimer Road, whereupon I immediately recognised the terraced house where I had been born. The window was dressed with pure white curtains made from lace, the front door was newly painted green, the doorstep shone with the application of Cardinal red polish.

Much to our surprise our new mam was not at the house to meet us, so Peter and I decided to go and explore outside. The old toilets were still stacked in the yard. We peered into the window of the plumber's shop, there was no-one there, it looked as though it was just being used for storage.

The yard seemed claustrophobic after coming from the country. The garden walls on either side rose like giant sentries guarding the property. They were so tall it was impossible to see over them. Peter and I had a good try to scale up the walls but we were unsuccessful. The only available toilet was a small brick monstrosity with a slate roof, that housed an old-fashioned toilet bowl, covered with a large long wooden seat. There were squares of newspaper threaded with string hanging on a nail, to represent toilet paper. This was so archaic in comparison to The Cottages.

We decided that it was quite boring outside in the yard and decided to go indoors. The living room had been newly decorated, two new armchairs sat either side of the fireplace. The shelf and sideboard were now adorned with delicate ornaments, made from porcelain. We were impatient, we either wanted to meet this new mam or go out into the street to play. Dad decided that the latter would be best for us, I supposed to get us out from under his feet.

Nonchalantly kicking a ball against the front wall of the house, I suddenly felt eyes burning into the back of my neck. Turning slightly I could see a woman out of the corner of my eye leaning against a coach built pram, in which lay a small child. I pretended not to notice her and carried on kicking the ball. Eventually the woman spoke enquiring as to whether we were Pearl and Peter Roberts. We assured her that we were. "Well, I'm your dad's new wife," she ventured and pointed to the baby in the pram. Then she dropped her bombshell, "And this is your baby brother, David."

Cautiously eyeing both of us, she indicated that we bore no resemblance to our dad, and that we must look like our mother had looked. She then added, "I hope that you are both going to behave yourselves. I've enough on my plate without looking after naughty kids. I've only taken you both for your dad's sake." If we had thought we were going to be greeted with affection, then we were very sadly disappointed. On the other hand, if she thought that she was getting malleable children, then she was going to be disappointed too. Warning signals, sounded in my mind, "watch out for that woman," they seemed to say, with a maturity way above my nine years.

We followed her into the house, Peter helping her to lift the baby's pram over the step. "A right little gentleman aren't we?" she said sarcastically. Peter and I glanced at each other, it was obvious that she was not going to give us a chance. Once 'Mam' had settled the baby, she beckoned us to go up the stairs to show us our sleeping arrangements. Peter was to sleep in the front room. My room was to be the box room. A small room at the rear of the house. To gain admittance to this room, it was necessary to walk through another bedroom. This other bedroom was occupied by my dad and this new mam along with baby David. Once out of earshot of my dad , this woman turned to Peter and I, and informed us never to call her 'Mam'. "My name's Grace," she said. "So call me Grace. Not Aunt, Not Mam, just Grace. You're not my kids, I'm just looking after you." This prospect quite pleased me, I didn't like this woman, she had a thin face with mean lips.

The small bedroom which I was led into did nothing to cheer me. It was sparsely furnished, with a single bed, and a chest of drawers which had a marble top on which stood a wash bowl and jug. The floor was covered in threadbare linoleum on which lay a handmade peg rug, made of rags from old clothes. The lighting was dim, consisting of a low wattage bulb without a shade. The whole atmosphere was gloomy, and did nothing to improve my mood. The small casement window overlooked the plumber's yard.

Peter was quite satisfied with his room, it was quite spacious and overlooked the street. There was a spare single bed in there for when David was older.

The following day, Grace took me down the road to the local rag and bone merchants, where I was rigged out with clothes for school, chosen from smelly piles of rags taken from a skip. The Rag and Bone man had collected the old clothes from house to house calls. He could be seen with his horse and cart shouting, "Rag bone! Any old rag bone! Good prices paid, any old rag bone!"

People would run out of their homes, with a pile of old clothes, which they sold to him for just a few coppers or a goldfish. I was really upset at the prospect of having to wear these clothes, even in The Cottage Homes the clothes may have been passed down, but they were clean. I sulked all the way back to the house.

Back inside, Grace began to show her true colours. "You ungrateful little tow rag. Do you think we have money to burn? If you think that you are going to have new clothes, you are sadly mistaken, this stuff is plenty good enough for you." She slapped my face with every word that she uttered. "Now get up those stairs and stay there until you can learn to be grateful." She threw open the staircase door and kicked me up each step. The expression on her face was one of pure evil. Welcome home, Pearl, I thought.

Grace allowed me to come down the stairs in time for my dad's return from work. "How's she doing?" enquired my dad beckoning towards me.

"Oh she's fine. We've been shopping today, for new school clothes for her. We bought them from the money which you gave me last night." Grace lied. "Both the kids are off to school tomorrow."

I wanted to tell my dad that Grace had lied to him about the clothes and that she had beaten me, but something held me back, a warning in my head told me to hold my council.

Peter received as many beatings as myself, though he was more resilient than I and would fight back kicking and screaming. He also made every attempt to protect me without much success, screaming, "Leave her alone, you old hag." This did nothing at all to favour his cause, and he would receive even more ferocious beatings.

Everywhere that Peter went I went also. "Need to keep an eye on you Pearly Pellard," he'd say. I also became a goodies ticket for him. Down to the park we would go, where numerous lads gathered around the bowling pavilion. Peter would make me take my pants down and charge each of the spectators a twopence to have a look of my bare tummy. I had no idea what the lads found so interesting or why they should want to look at my tummy. He gave me a halfpenny for each twopence he received. "Only fair I should get more, being your manager and all," he would say. At the time I saw no wrong in what we were doing, and it made Peter happy.

One day when I came home from school there was a police officer sitting in the living room. Peter had been to visit his godmother, and whilst there had stolen money from her purse. Charges were brought against him and he was sent off to a remand home. I suppose he carried out the theft because neither of us were given any pocket money, the only money he had was from my little circus act.

Grace was very pleased that she had rid herself of one of us, she was under the mistaken illusion that I would be easier to manage on my own, but she had a rude awakening for Peter had been a good tutor.

I had found a good source of income. My dad was a Bookie's runner, a person who accepted bets for the local turf accountant. Street gambling was illegal so my dad would leave a leather pouch containing betting slips and money in a leather drawstring pouch, behind the back gate in the entry for collection by the bookie. Once a week I would help myself to sixpence, which I would spend on chips and penny ice-lollipops. I could not buy sweets or chocolates because these were still on ration and I did not have any coupons. Sometimes my dad and the Bookie had terrible rows and I often wondered whether it was over the missing sixpences. It was very fortunate for me that no-one ever discovered my thefts.

In the summer I would go to the Grace Road cricket ground, collect the empty lemonade bottles then take them back to the shops and get a penny back on each bottle. When the rose-hips were ripe I'd spend hours collecting them and take them to the pharmacist, where I'd sell them for a few pence.

David my baby brother was now beginning to toddle. One day he hung onto my leg to steady himself. Grace began to scream like a mad woman. "Don't touch that girl, she's filthy, she's just a thing!" From then on David was taught to call me 'Thing', and I was never allowed to touch the child again. This hurt me deeply as I genuinely loved the little boy.

During this time, life was jogging along at school. "Today children, we are going to make a paper boat," my form teacher instructed. "If the boats are successful, you may take the one you have made home." Unfortunately, mine was a complete disaster. The glue wouldn't stick, and the sail fell off. In fact the boat just looked like scrap paper, much to the amusement of the other children in the form. It was obvious that I didn't get to take mine home. On leaving school that afternoon, a boy from my form named Donald caught up with me. He was a clean tidy boy, each day he would wear a brilliant white shirt to school, his hair always looked slick, brushed down with Brylcreem. "Here Pearl, have my boat, I don't want it, I have a wooden boat, which I float on the canal." His paper boat had been made to perfection and he had painted it in blue and red watercolours. If only Donald could have known what trouble his boat was to bring.

Carrying the boat carefully home, I thought up a cunning plan. I would tell Grace that I had made it as a gift for David; she might like me a little then and allow me to play with my brother. Rushing into the house holding the boat aloft I chanted, "Look what I've made. Look what I've made!" Grace narrowed her spiteful eyes and took the boat from my hands. Examining it closely she shouted, "You rotten little liar, you didn't make this it's far too neat for anything that you could have made. Go on admit it, you've stolen it haven't you? Tomorrow we will go to the school together, to find out the truth."

"No please don't," I begged. "I lied, Donald from my form gave it to me. I didn't pinch the boat, honest."

"You wouldn't know honesty if it looked you in the face," Grace said with sarcasm.

In the morning Grace did not mention the boat. Phew, I thought, I've got away with it and happily went off to school. Half way through the morning Grace appeared at the classroom door, accompanied by the Headmaster. "Donald! Pearl! I want you both in my office, now!" Once inside the room he asked, "Is this your boat Donald?"

"Yes Sir," replied Donald.

"Did you give the boat to Pearl?" Donald looked over at me, his cheeks flushed with embarrassment. Lowering his eyes he replied, "No Sir, it was stolen." Hardly believing my ears, I protested. "That's just not true Sir! Donald gave the boat to me." No-one believed me, Donald was a model pupil, I was just a scruffy untidy girl, who chatted a lot in class, often causing disruption.

On returning to the classroom, my form teacher commanded, "Stand on your desk Pearl, your classmates wish to look at you." Then she told the whole class, that I was a thief and a liar. I stood there for the rest of the day. Donald could not meet my eyes, refusing to even look at me. I stared at him in defiance because I knew the truth.

Frightened to go home, but knowing I must, I sidled cautiously into the kitchen. I jumped back in terror as an arm shot out from behind the door and grabbed me by the hair. "Got you, you lying bitch." Grace had been lying in wait for my return. She tossed me onto the floor, and with her knee pressed into my chest, to hold me down, she forced open my mouth, and filled it with carbolic soap, pushing the soap deep into my throat, causing me to retch. "That will teach you to lie and steal, you apology for a human being." Next, I was being pulled across the kitchen floor by my hair, I could feel the stone tiles grazing my legs, the warm blood pouring from my nose. Grace yanked me into a standing position in front of the sink and ducked my head and face into freezing cold water, which took my breath away. I could barely breathe and could feel myself losing consciousness. I must have eventually blacked out, for the next thing I recall was lying on my bed in a darkened room.

Grace was shaking me. "Here's your dinner brat. You don't deserve it, I wish you would starve to death, then the world would be a happier place." The meal consisted of bread and weak brown gravy. I could feel that my eyes and lips were swollen, but Grace felt no remorse at what she had done to me. Taking the plate from her hands, I dared not meet her eyes, in this individual I had certainly met my match. I thought back to Ma at the Cottage Homes. I could almost visualise Ma as a fairy godmother in comparison to this evil woman.

My dad was oblivious to anything that was going on in the household. He went to work, came home, ate his dinner, then dressed himself up in his best suit complete with carnation in the lapel, and went to the pub. Come closing time, he would come home blind drunk singing army songs. Often I would lie in bed, listening to Grace and dad arguing. They would always make up, then I would hear them noisily making love through the thin walls. Although at that age it was not evident to me what they were doing. I assumed that they were playing games. Sometimes I wished enviously that they would play games with me.

In the summer holidays I was always awoken at six in the morning, made to get out of bed, clean my room, then scrub the kitchen floor on my hands and knees. I was given a sparse breakfast, then made to wash myself in cold water. Come eight o'clock, I was given two slices of bread and butter and a bottle of tap water and ordered to go to the local park. I was instructed not to leave the park under any circumstances and not to return to the house until six o'clock in the evening. Every so many hours, Grace would come to the park to check that I was still there.

Grace cleaned houses for the rich folk of Aylestone Park, and I soon learned what times she attended each house. The park keeper must have been sick to his back teeth of me asking him, "What's the time, Mister?" If the time coincided with 'one of her houses' as she called them, I would nip off and do my own thing, then rush back to the park in time for her patrol.

On one such occasion, I had eaten my bread and butter and was absolutely starving of hunger, when I spotted a display of Horlick tablets stacked up in their little square tins outside the local Grocery store. Shiftily looking around me, quick as a flash my hand shot out and took two tins, which I shoved up my elasticated knickers leg, then back to the park where I sat and noshed the contents of both tins at once in order to hide the evidence. I spent the rest of the afternoon in the park toilets being sick.

It was abysmal when it rained. I would go straight to the park and take cover in the shelter, having to stay there all day, I dared not go off on one of my escapades for fear of getting wet, then Grace would know my little secret. The only company I had on these days were old men, sometimes they were very dubious characters. Those wet days dragged on as if they were an eternity.

It was during this summer that the fair arrived, setting up their rides on the park. They lived in their gaily-painted caravans, and had horses tethered up outside their doors. The fair-people soon came to know me, I was the only child in the park at eight o'clock in the morning. One morning, I befriended one of the gypsy girls, her name was Isla. We quickly became the best of friends. Her family was very kind to me allowing me to share in their meals. My favourite meal was always breakfast, rashers of bacon with fried egg. This was a luxury beyond belief. Sometimes they would give me a free ride on the dodgem cars, and on one occasion I rode the big wheel, Isla and I were the only fares. Each morning I would wait with bated breath, in case Grace kept me from going to the park, but she was only too pleased to be rid of me. Isla's father enquired about the bruises on my arms and face. When I explained to him that my stepmother had made them, he wanted to call the police. I pleaded with him not to do so. "It will only make matters worse for me, Mister," I told him.

That evening there was a knock at the door, there stood a police officer. "Can I come inside please." I heard him say to Grace. "There has been a complaint, that you are ill treating your stepdaughter, and that she is badly bruised." Grace's eyes narrowed, as I cowered further into my chair. "That is not true, Pearl has been up to her tricks again. We have a terrible time with her, she tells such terrible lies." The policeman turned to me and asked where I had got my visible bruises from. "Fell down the stairs Mister," was my frightened reply. I just dared not tell the truth, for fear of further reprisal. The policeman appeared satisfied, he gave me a warning about telling lies and left. Grace went spare. "That's the last time you go out this holiday," she said, and I again received one of her beatings.

The following morning when I awoke I did not have to wait long to find out what was in store for me. "You will spend the rest of your holidays in the cellar. I can't have you hanging around me all day." She opened the cellar door and sent me down the stairs with a book and my bread and butter sandwiches. I spent the rest of the summer holidays, ten hours each day, in the cellar. I would tap on the cellar grating at children playing above. After explaining to them that they must keep my being in the cellar a secret, they would bring me apples that they had scrumped from the big house on the corner, chop them up and push them through the grill on the grating. I would eat core, pip and all to hide the evidence. It became obvious that Grace did find out about my exploits and explained the situation away to the neighbours by telling them that I was a raindrop short of a puddle, using my mother's mental illness as a springboard for people to question my sanity.

The hardest part of being locked up was that I couldn't get out to do my 'little jobs' to supplement the sixpence a week I pinched from the Bookie.

One day at school, some children, led by a girl named Beryl began to taunt me. They formed a circle around me then began to chant. "Your mam's in the loony bin," they chanted, on and on laughing and prodding as they chanted. Trying to defend my mother's name I shouted, "She's not in a loony bin; she's dead, my dad told me." The chanting continued, when suddenly something snapped inside of me, a blind rage overtook my whole being. Grabbing hold of the ringleader, Beryl, I began to punch her over and over again. She fell to the floor, and blood started to trickle from her ear. An ambulance arrived and took Beryl away. I was terrified, what had I done? Had I killed her? The Headmaster immediately suspended me from school. My form teacher escorted me home. Going into the house, he explained the incident to Grace. She seemed highly delighted that the incident had occurred, I was not even thrashed. "You're done for, this time," she gloated. "It's the remand home for you, with your brother. Rotten to the core the pair of you," she continued.

The following day, the Headmaster and the school

governors convened a meeting, which Grace and I were to attend. On arrival we also found Beryl's mother there, but still no sign of Beryl. Perhaps she's dead, I thought. The meeting began. Beryl's mother explained that Beryl had got a mastoid at the back of the ear, that my heavy punches had caused complications, that an operation had been performed, and that Beryl was now making a good recovery.

"Now Pearl," asked the Head, "What's your story?" At which stage I proceeded to explain about the taunting, outlining the dreadful things which Beryl had said about my mother. Beryl's mother looked shocked. Hesitating a little before she spoke, she explained that Beryl must have overheard a recent conversation held between a neighbour and herself. "Why did you tell your neighbour that my mother was a loony?" I rudely interrupted. The Head held up his hand.

"Pearl, your mother is not dead. She is in fact in a mental institution. You were told a falsehood to protect you." I was stunned. My mother a loony. I'd never live it down. The Headmaster went on to say, that because of the unusual circumstances surrounding the situation, and taking into consideration the cruelty of the other children towards me, if Beryl's mother was in agreement, he was prepared to drop the matter. Everyone nodded in agreement, and much to Grace's annoyance I was reinstated into the school. "You're going to pay for this in some way," sneered Grace on the way home. "I'll think of something." There was no doubt in my mind that she would.

The evenings were now dark, the nights were cold. Coke fires were being lit in the hearth. This meant that I would have to collect the coke from the Gas Works. At four thirty each Saturday morning, I was roughly shaken awake by Grace. Pulling on my clothes which consisted of vest, pants, black skirt, thin jumper, short socks, navy gabardine mac and Wellington boots, and with my head covered in an old tartan scarf sewed up to form a bonnet, I was sent out of the house, pushing a handmade rough wooden wheel barrow. My hands would be frozen as I trundled up the road, trying hard to keep the wheel barrow on course.

After about ten minutes I would arrive at the Gas Works, where a long queue would already have formed. Mostly the queue consisted of men. They would stand and moan, "When's this bloody coke coming off ration?"

"Sick of this caper, every Saturday morning."

I'd stand there and cheekily retort, "Well at least you've got trousers on, and a big coat." Most of the men wore their great army coats. Nattering amongst themselves, I often heard them say, "Whoever sends that young girl out on her own at this time of morning, in those clothes, wants shooting." I presumed that they were talking about me, because they would give me a cup of hot tea from the flasks that they had brought with them. After about two hours it would be my turn to be served. The men at the weighbridge would place the bag of coke into my barrow, I would hand over the money and start to trundle home. The journey was always tiresome, the wheels would not go where

I wanted them to. They were only made from old buckled wheels from a child's cycle. The barrow was so heavy, it caused me to have blisters on my already freezing hands. Often the barrow would tip up, spilling the coke onto the pavement. I would stand and pick every morsel up, as I was sure that Grace knew exactly how many pieces should be in a bag. Passers-by often gave me a hand up and the Milkman would shout, "On the coke run again Pearly?" Then he would give me a drink of milk. It seemed that all the people in the district sympathised with me, even the local Chippie gave me the scratchings left over from his fried fish.

I would arrive home exhausted, but still receive no thanks, just a round of bread and dripping and a cup of hot water. Grace said that hot water kept the innards clean.

Feeling very weary after the early rise, I still went to Miss Bird's shop next door to help her, which didn't worry me, it was better than having to spend time with Grace.

It was obvious that I always looked a sorry sight, for Mrs Berry from down the road, came knocking on the door one day. She had three daughters, all slightly older than me, these girls were dressed beautifully. She handed over a large bag of dresses. "These will fit Pearly nicely, my girls have grown out of them." The dresses were lovely, all sorts of colours, materials and designs. I was really looking forward to wearing them. "You don't think you're having these do you? These dresses are for normal girls, not trash like you." This was Grace being spiteful again. Within days, Grace had sold the dresses to a second-hand shop. Oh how I wished so much to be normal, then I could wear nice clothes like the Berry girls. I wasn't sure why I was abnormal, but Grace kept telling me that I was, therefore I began to believe her. Although, I couldn't see any difference between me and other people, with the exception of my unruly hair, which I must admit did get messy. I spent an awful lot of time studying the matter.

The most memorable gifts that I received were a coach built doll's pram and a German lifelike porcelain doll, which my Auntie Elsie had treasured since her own childhood. She felt that it was appropriate for me to have it, being the daughter of her sister. I was so thrilled that I walked them around the streets straight away, feeling so proud. I'd never owned anything quite so magnificent. The following day they had gone missing, Grace had sold them splitting the money between herself and my father, his for ale, and she bought herself a new coat. I was heart broken. On another occasion a nearby neighbour gave me a second-hand blue Raleigh bicycle, with a wicker basket attached to the handle bars. I was thrilled to my bones with it, the world would be my oyster with this bicycle. I could almost feel the wind in my face as I sped along the canal tow path, but alas this was not to be. "You can keep the bike, if you can tell me how many acorns grow on a horse chestnut tree," sneered Grace. I flew to the park and almost skidded to a halt underneath the nearest acorn tree, and started the impossible task of trying to count the acorns. "Hello Pearl, what are we up to today then?" The park keepers all knew my name because of how often I frequented the park.

"Hi Parkie, how many acorns grow on that tree, it's a matter of life and death," I told him. Laughingly he went to great lengths to explain about the seasons and how different amounts grew each year. This was a truly difficult poser, I'd just have to guess and hope Grace would believe me. Dashing back home I said, "Grace I've counted the acorns, there are two thousand and three," I told her proudly. Of course the answer should have been none, the acorn being a fruit of the mighty oak. The next day my beautiful blue bicycle was missing and I never did get to ride it, not even once.

Shortly before my eleventh birthday I was to sit my eleven plus examination. My form teacher informed Grace that I was bright and could attain enough marks to attend the Grammar school. On hearing this she grabbed me by the hair, pulling my head back, she looked into my eyes and said, "You pass that exam and I will break your neck. Just make sure that you fail, we are not paying out on any posh uniform for you. Just get any ideas about going to the Grammar school, out of your head." So that put the scupper on that.

On the day of the eleven plus, I assembled in the school hall along with the other children. Taking our seats, we were given our instructions for the morning's work. I picked up my pen, then Grace's words came rushing back to me. I purposely answered each question incorrectly. Sometime later when the results were issued, I was found to have one of the lowest marks ever obtained.

So it was the local Comprehensive school for me, Grace was elated with the results, especially knowing that it had been her threats that had made me fail. I compensated myself with the fact that I would not have to do miles of homework, like some girls I knew who already attended the Grammar school.

CHAPTER EIGHT

The school buzzed with excitement, it was the last day of the summer term, also the last day at junior school for my classmates and I.

The walls were stripped of our achievements, which had decorated the walls of the classroom for most of the term. I had painted two of the pictures on display but threw them into the waste paper bin, knowing that I would not receive any recognition for them from anyone at home. The other children were all discussing their forthcoming trips to the seaside. They were going to travel on the train to such seaside resorts as Skegness. All except me. I was filled with dread at the prospect of spending six whole weeks in the clutches of Grace. Especially after the previous summer in the cellar.

However, this time fate was to be on my side. Only three days into the holiday, I was awoken in the middle of the night, being violently shaken by Grace. She stood in tears, as she told me that David was to be admitted to hospital. "He's desperately ill, I don't know when I shall see you, just fend for yourself," she said.

Today was my eleventh birthday, there was no recognition of this, with no presents or birthday cards. In my childish mind I thought that God had given me a gift, by admitting David to hospital, thus allowing me to roam freely.

At first light, I was up and dressed, ate my breakfast

and left the house. I made my way to my friend Joyce Pitt's house. Her parents owned the local Greengrocers shop. I skipped up the road, with my skipping rope, to find Joyce's mother setting up her stall outside the shop. "You are an early bird Pearl," said Mrs Pitt, "Joyce is still in bed. Help me to set up the stall while you wait."

At last Joyce emerged, "Coming down the back waters to play? I asked. These where the streams across the playing fields near the canal, where we fished for tiddlers, with nets made of bamboo canes and stocking tops. We put our catches into jam jars, with string tied around the rim to carry the jars home. Of course Joyce had to care for mine otherwise Grace would have known where I had been.

We played the cruel game of frog racing. Taking a large bobbin of shoe twine we wound the twine around the frogs legs, then lowered them into the water, the poor frogs swam like mad to get to the other side, thinking they were going to escape. Once there we rewound the reel, pulling the frogs in like a haul of fish. Those poor frogs, children are so cruel. I shouldn't think that they were any good for anything else when we had finished with them.

We returned to Mrs Pitt's shop at lunchtime, where she fed us with home made vegetable soup, made with vegetables from her shop and large slices of crusty bread, this was always washed down with a glass of Tizer or Dandelion and Burdock. These delicious offerings were such treats for me. After literally licking the plate clean Mrs Pitt said, "that will be sixpence

Pearl," then she would break into a raucous laugh. Instead I washed the dishes for her.

In the afternoon we played scissors and strides and hopscotch in the street, with Joyce's brother and sister, it was a perfect day.

The following morning Grace informed me that she would be visiting the hospital every day, until David recovered. He had caught a nasty disease from the old toilets in the back yard, he was very ill, and was being kept in isolation. What bliss. I cruelly hoped that David would stay in the hospital forever, allowing me eternal freedom. From that day on, Joyce and I roamed freely. Some days we would walk to Bradgate Park. We would picnic among the fern, climb Old John, and paddle in the stream. We would chase deer across the hills and get reprimanded by the park rangers. Another time whilst fishing in the back waters of the Aylestone playing fields a man approached us, and asked if he could take our photograph. "Hello, I am the man from the "Leicester Mercury", this is the local rag for Leicestershire. I'm doing an article on children and their activities during the school holidays. You pair seem to be having a good time, hold up your jam jar." He clicked away with his camera. How exciting Joyce and I thought, our picture in the newspaper for everyone to see, we thought it a great honour and fancied ourselves as local celebrities.

The following evening I returned from my play. Grace was back from the hospital and already waiting for me. "Where were you, yesterday?" she demanded to know.

"Down the back waters, with Joyce," I answered honestly. Smack, another nosebleed ensued. "What was that for?" I rudely asked.

"Talking to strange men. That's what that's for," she sneered. "Thought you were something special getting your face in the paper did you? Well you've done it for yourself now, there will be no more days out for you."

"Will you be going to the hospital tomorrow?" I ventured to ask. Thinking that once she'd gone I would nip out, returning home before she got back. She looked at me with mocking eyes, "I wasn't born yesterday, so don't get any fine ideas you lousy little scheming bitch." What did she mean?

The following morning I soon found out. I was awoken as usual at six a.m. Grace said, "Don't get dressed, get outside into the toilet and sit there for an hour, don't come in until you have been." This seemed a very strange order to me, never the less I went outside and tried to obey. Anyone who has ever been asked for a medical sample will know that it is virtually impossible to do even a drop of anything to order.

On returning into the house, I was dragged upstairs by the scruff of my neck and thrown into my room. A bread and butter sandwich, and a bottle of water stood on the dressing table. "Now stay there until I get back at teatime you apology for a person."

I could hear rustling on the other side of the door, and then Grace gave an evil laugh. As she retreated she shouted, "Get out of that one if you can filth." As soon as I was sure that Grace had left the house, I turned the large brass handle on my bedroom door, I pulled and nothing happened. I tugged and tugged again, it would not budge. What had she done, I wondered, there was no lock on the door. I resorted to kicking the door and screaming in temper, but no one heard. There was nothing left to do but sit on the bed. When my tears subsided my mind turned to how I was going to fill the day. I didn't have any books or toys in the room, in fact I didn't have any toys full stop. Eventually I turned my attention to the faded flowered wallpaper which adorned the bedroom walls. I began to count the flowers, then subtract, divide and multiply. After a few hours I was quite proficient.

Soon I needed desperately to pee, what was I going to do? I strutted the room with legs plaited together, the urge was becoming unbearable, my tummy pained enormously with the fullness of my bladder. After about an hour a sudden notion came into my head. That's it, I thought, I would pee into the water jug on the dresser, and throw the urine out of the window, it was a far better bet than peeing myself, Grace would have gone bananas. Taking the large jug I did what I had to do and took care to wipe the jug clean on the pegged rag rug.

I decided that's what I will have to do on each emergency when I am locked in the room, I thought it was a brilliant idea and solved any immediate problem. In any event Grace must have thought that I was a camel and could store my water.

I'd counted the wallpaper for too long now. I was bored, what else could I do? After a flash of inspiration,

I started to talk to myself. "Ha, that's it, I shall make some dollies." I collected quite a nice pile of tiny pieces from the rug. "I must be careful in case Grace notices any bits missing. I must keep the dollies small and then hide them well." This is how I spoke to myself. I tried in vain to make the small bits of rags stick together, but they were too small to tie. Then I had a brain wave, I could use the mucous from my nose. Thus I got to work, and within no time at all, I had made three dolls each measuring a quarter of an inch tall. Once hardened, the dolls were fine. I gave each one a name Peter Rug, Pauly Rug and Penny Rug. I told them magical fairy stories, which I had made up myself, and pretended that this hovel of a bedroom was a magical kingdom. I soon learned to lose myself inside my mind, I could walk on the beach at the seaside or ride the fairground rides, dance in the meadows and make daisy chains. My imagination became so vivid, that most people would have diagnosed me as a demented child, to me I was just keeping my mind occupied, my imagination was far too fertile to lay idle. It was just my way out of a difficult and lonely existence.

When I heard the key in the front lock, I carefully hid the dolls under the damaged linoleum at the back of my bed, knowing that they would be safe from Grace, for I always cleaned my own room. Then I just lay there feigning sleep. I was getting as crafty as a cart-load of monkeys, always trying to outwit Grace.

When Grace came to let me out of the bedroom, there was again much rustling from the other side of the bedroom door. Once the door was opened, I inspected the outside of the door, where I found a strong pyjama cord tied to the brass knob, and then attached to a heavy trunk, which held the door firm. Grace followed my eyes, noticing that I had figured out her 'locking device'. "Clever hey," she said sniggering, just as though the whole thing was a huge joke. Again I thought of how much I hated this horrid woman, her sole source of pleasure appeared to come from what new tortures she could dream up for me.

It was the same ritual every day for the rest of the holidays, with the exception of Saturdays and Sundays, when my dad stayed home from work.

Each day I did my counting and each day I made dolls, until I had thirty in all. I would enter into daydreams, making up stories of handsome princes and courtiers, my dolls would be part of the scene. Each day seemed such a long, long time. Sometimes I could hear children playing in the street, their happy laughter rang out grating on my very being, causing such deep envy because of the difference in circumstances. I so wanted to be outside with them and join in their games, that I could feel the hurt deep in the pit of my stomach, and would sob uncontrollably. Never before had I felt such deep envy.

There was a haberdashery shop called F. & G. Birds next door to our house, which was run by a middle-aged spinster. She was a woman of some breeding. On Saturdays she would allow me to help her in the shop. She sold almost everything including liberty bodices, vests, thick Lyle stockings, hats, knitting wools and much, much more.

Each Saturday she scrubbed me from top to bottom, until I shone, "can't have you serving in my shop looking like some waif and stray," she tutted. I then changed into what she called my shop clothes, which she provided and washed and pressed each week. "There spick and span, ready for work Pearly," was her weekly comment. "It's the best I can do for you, it's not possible to make a silk purse out of a sow's ear," she'd say eyeing me critically. My duties were to dust and tidy the shelves, straighten up the wares, make sure there was plenty of brown paper available and open and close the door for the customers, thanking them for coming and shopping with us. There was a cash box that slid on wires around the shop, worked by a pulley which ended its journey in Miss Bird's living room. Sometimes I was allowed to put the money into the small tube which was then placed onto the overhead pulley and pull the cord, it made me very excited when the tube whizzed away out of sight.

Most Saturdays I would do the 'chicken run', as Miss Bird called it. This entailed running to Miss Bird's brother's house, (his real name was Dickey), to deliver stale food and potato peelings to him for his chickens. I would run fast, to allow me more time when I got there, where he'd sit me on a tall stool in his kitchen and give me a glass of milk and two biscuits. "For your trouble," Dickey would say. Then hens would run around the kitchen, and strut on top of his Welsh Dresser, clucking away at the sight of a stranger in their kitchen. Mr Bird had a name for all of his hens. On one of these runs Miss Bird put a large tin of unopened biscuits into the carrier bag for me to deliver, and my curiosity got the better of me. I went into an entry on the way to her brother's and opened up the tin, to reveal an array of brightly wrapped chocolate biscuits. The temptation was far too great; I hadn't eaten breakfast and was hungry, I'm sure Dickey Bird's hens wouldn't miss a few. I must have devoured at least six of the biscuits before I realised that they were mouldy. Normally after my visit I would run straight back to the shop to resume my duties, but on this day I had to stop twice to be sick, then I felt queasy for the remainder of the day, not daring to tell anyone why, my own greed had punished me.

Miss Bird used to tell me that she had known my mother. She'd say, "Your mother was from good breeding my girl, not like your father's new wife, she's common." This would make me feel warm inside knowing that my mother had been better than Grace. If for no other reason than this, I liked Miss Bird immensely.

Most of the children in the district were in awe of Miss Bird. If they loitered in the small vestibule that fronted her shop, she'd rush out with her sweeping brush shouting, "Shoo, you will break my doorstep." The children would run away sniggering behind their hands. The neighbours all thought it was somewhat of an enigma why Miss Bird took to a waif like me, yet could not tolerate any other child.

Each Saturday she would give me a golden coloured threepenny piece, and six hard-boiled sweets. I would hide these up my knickers' leg, which fortunately were very ample and reinforced with very strong elastic. Miss Bird's shop can still be seen today as it was then, in the Leicester Costume Museum. Saturday was surely my very best day of the whole week.

On Sundays I would attend afternoon Sunday School, where we would be taught Bible stories and sing hymns. Each Sunday we would be given a stamp of a religious icon to stick on a card to prove that we had attended.

One Sunday there was to be a Regatta on the Aylestone canal. It was quite an event, all of my school friends were going to attend. "Can I have the afternoon off from Sunday School please, Grace?" I asked.

"No you bloody well can't," came the acid reply. However, a plan of action had already formed in my mind. I knew that her and my Dad always went to bed on a Sunday afternoon. "Need the bloody rest after looking after a rotten little pig like you all week," Grace often informed me, so I knew it was a sure thing.

With my stamp stuck safely on my card, I had the decency to sing one hymn, '*All things bright and beautiful*', then I sat down and leant back against my chair. "Anything wrong Pearl?" enquired the Sunday School mistress. "Yes Miss, I feel faint."

"You had better go home then, walk slowly the air will do you good." Once outside I ran like the wind, galloping down to the canal, I hoped that I had not missed anything. Everything was splendid, the boats were so colourful, decorated with ribbons, there was a brass band playing and the Cafe was serving teas, cakes and ices. The collection had not been taken when I'd left the church, so I had a penny to spend and bought a penny orange iced lolly. There I was ambling along, profusely sucking my lolly, when a hand grabbed me on the shoulder. "Got you," said the familiar voice of Grace, her presence had definitely not been included in my plan. Putting her foot out she tripped me up, badly grazing my knee on the rough towpath. "Now get off home with you. Get out the scrubbing brush and bucket and scrub the yard." My dad wondered what I was doing, but after explaining my adventures of that afternoon, he told me that the punishment fitted the crime.

That day I scrubbed the yard until dusk, my already grazed knees were very sore. I really felt sorry for myself. The deception of my feigned illness at the Sunday School had not paid off at all. That would teach me to tell lies in the church.

CHAPTER NINE

Hurrah! The first morning has arrived for my attendance at my new school, Sir Jonathan North, Girls school, which is about one and a half miles from my home. I have been to the rag and bone yard to be fitted out with my uniform, which consists of a navy tunic, a supposedly white blouse and a navy blazer. It is impossible to say that I look smart. Eight o'clock arrives and I am raring to go. "What are you in such a hurry for?" Grace asks.

"I've got to be there by nine o'clock, I don't want to be late on my first day." I respond excitedly. "Leave here at ten minutes to nine, plenty of time for you," Grace said. I must now run so fast, I can hardly get my breath. When I arrive at the school at ten minutes past nine, the playground is empty. I wander into the school, and am immediately spotted by a teacher. "Late on your first day, what's your name girl?" she asked.

"Pearl Roberts, Miss," I answered. She ran her finger down a register that she held in her hands and located my name. "Yes, bottom form, first year, third door on your right! Mrs Palmer. If you cannot be early on your first morning, you will be in the bottom form for the rest of your school life."

"Yes, Miss," I mumbled, scurrying off. Under my breath, I spat, "I hate you Grace, it's all your fault." Every morning from then on I ran all the way to school, usually arriving ten minutes late, so that each morning I had to face the form mistress's sarcasm. "What excuse is it this morning Pearl?" she would enquire. I would just shrug and sit down, after all there was no way I could change the situation so it would just have to remain the same.

On that first morning I had put my head around the classroom door. Thirty pairs of eyes turned towards me, thirty girls dressed in bright new uniforms, and there I stood looking completely dishevelled, masses of blond curly hair tangled on top of my head, socks around my ankles and a dingy white blouse. What a sight I must have looked.

Mrs Palmer stood and looked at me in dismay. "You must be Roberts," she said at last, after the initial shock of my appearance had worn off. Pointing to my attire she said, "Is that the best you can do?"

"Yes Miss, I mumbled feeling ashamed.

"Sit next to that girl there, the one with the plaits." I sat down and turned to look at my desk mate, she is a pretty very short girl, with very blue eyes and long plaited hair. "What's your name?" I asked.

"Pamela Clarbour," she replied. I know when I look at her that she will be my very best friend. I feel there is something infinite and enduring about her. I see the steadiness of her eyes, she is not seeing my clothes or my appearance, she is seeing me.

The lessons began and I could hardly believe what I was hearing, some of the girls were finding reading difficult. We changed classrooms to take mathematics. The girls began to recite their two, three and four times tables, some of the girls were finding this subject difficult too. I can divide and multiply very large numbers, thanks to the flowered wallpaper in my bedroom. I started to get bored and began to talk and fidget. "Shut up Roberts, it is no wonder that you received such low marks in your eleven plus, if today's behaviour is anything to go by," the maths teacher chided. Her name was Miss Wright.

"I can do these tables, standing on my head, and divide and multiply," I rudely remarked. She took up my challenge. "In that case, let me see you try these questions." Much to the amusement of my classmates. She scribbled away on the blackboard. "Now answer these," Miss Wright beckoned. She was looking smug. I stared at the blackboard for a few moments, picked up the chalk and scribbled down the answers. Miss Wright is looking at me in amazement. You have them all correct." She was now firing mental arithmetic questions at me, I got nine of the ten questions right. "I'm puzzled, why did you get such low marks in your eleven plus examination?" she asks. Lying, I told her that I was ill on the day of the exams, and could not concentrate. Within two months I had jumped two forms and was placed in alpha stream, the top set. I came within the top ten in the form at each test examination I took thereafter, except for needlework, which I just could not do at all. The needle just would not go where I wanted it to. School was not going too badly at all, not like life at home and I relished every day that I was there.

David was now home from the hospital, but still attended as a day patient. Grace said that I could not go straight home from school, because she could not trust me with a key. I must stay out of the house until six o'clock. I must not play because I was wearing my school uniform. Which of course I totally ignored.

Pamela, whose name was shortened to Pam, invited me back to her house where she made me dripping sandwiches, she commented that she has never seen anyone eat so many rounds of bread in her life. Her mum and dad liked me and treated me well, I guess they felt a little sorry for me, taking into consideration my appearance. It is almost certain that the food which her parents fed me, kept me fit because Grace's idea of a staple diet was still mostly bread and gravy.

Pam soon became my confidante and I tell her all about Grace, everyone has to have someone that they can confide the dark shadows of their mind to. She often finds my stories difficult to believe but knows they must be true because I show Pam the heavy bruising, always begging her not to tell her parents or anyone else for that matter, it must remain our secret. It would only cause even more bother and beatings for me. Grace was always trying to think up evil new schemes to torment me, if she knew that I had been gossiping about these schemes they would only become more horrific.

Summer turned to winter and with the end of term, school broke up to celebrate Christmas. The school buzzed with excitement, everyone was anticipating their Christmas presents. I remained silent, I had no illusions of what mine would be, an apple and an orange if I was lucky. I wished everyone a Happy Christmas and began to pack my satchel, Pam shyly walked up to me and gave me a small parcel, "It's not much," she said. "We have not got a lot of money." I took the parcel with thanks and walked away to open it otherwise Grace would confiscate its contents. Wrapped neatly inside was a bright yellow propelling pencil, with a silk tassel on the end. I shall treasure it forever I vowed.

I was not going to Pam's house that afternoon, she had to go to a party with her mum. I wandered into the park, I knew I could not go home until six o'clock that evening. It was bitterly cold, my clothes were not really suitable for the freezing cold temperatures. The park was dark and deserted, all the other children had gone home to their warm fires. I ran around to keep myself warm, on my travels I saw a green electric generator house. Stopping to have a look, I noted the louvred sides to the house. "This is just the job," I said to myself. "I shall keep my pen in here. If I push it in the slat near the top, no-one will ever notice it." This was what I did and every time that I was allowed out I would go and take the pen out, carry it around with me all day, then take it back safely before returning home.

Many more little trinkets went into this place, it became my 'Treasure Holder', certainly different from keeping things in a dressing table drawer.

CHAPTER TEN

Christmas Day arrived. David had a pile of toys including a toy pedal car, a cowboy suit, and many more small items. I had an apple, an orange and an Enid Blyton book. Grace said I should be grateful, she seemed to think that I had received far more than I deserved. Dad didn't even seem to notice the differential in amounts, he was too busy boozing and was almost legless by Christmas dinner time. But at least I had a decent dinner for that day, and was not locked in my room, albeit that I had to walk the streets on Christmas afternoon, to allow Grace and Dad to have a sleep. The streets were deserted, peering through the windows as I walked I could see Christmas lights twinkling and children and parents playing with new board games. My jealousy was so deep, amid my tears I tried to will Grace to die, a truly horrible thing for a child to do. I was convinced that if she was in her grave I could be happy. Perhaps my Dad would then marry a kindly woman who could maybe love me. Once the two day Christmas festivities were over my Dad returned to work and there was still two whole weeks to get through before school began.

Once Dad had gone to work the usual early morning ritual began, toilet then locked in my room. Grace informed me that this is where I must stay for the duration of the holiday unless she needed any chores doing. At least I had my Enid Blyton book to read this time around. The snow lay heavily upon the ground. Grace decided to take David sledging on the canal, visit her sister then go to 'her houses'. "Get to the toilet before I go out," Grace ordered. She left me there for a whole hour in just my nightclothes, I was freezing cold, but still nature did not take its course. "Have you been yet!" Grace called.

"No I can't." This reply brought her dashing outside, she skidded to a halt at the toilet door.

"Get off now," she demanded. She grabbed my head and pushed my face into the lavatory bowl, flushing the toilet chain as she did so. I began to swallow the water from the toilet pan. Gagging and spluttering I kicked and screamed. The two old ladies who lived next door at number six came rushing round to see what all the commotion was about. Grace explained it all away with, "Just one of Pearl's tantrums again."

"You poor woman, having to put up with such behaviour," the old ladies sympathised, then they disappeared back into the warmth of their home. If only someone, anyone, would realise the truth I thought, but they didn't.

Once inside my bedroom, I heard the door being tied to the trunk with the rope again, and knew the house would soon be silent. At least while she was out, she couldn't torment me. Out came my little dolls, I pretended to teach poetry to them. I liked poetry and would often recite aloud and from memory in class, after all I had plenty of time to practice in my room.

After but a short time, this really strong urge to use the toilet started. It must have been the sprouts that I had noshed for Christmas dinner, my constitution wasn't used to the luxury of vegetables. It was okay when I wanted to pee, but what did I do now? I paced up and down the small room, my stomach ache becoming worse and worse. This was a real dilemma. I could not wait any longer, in a panic I grabbed the large water jug and used that. Then I began to sob, what was I going to do? After I had gained my self control, an idea came into my head. Underneath my bedroom window lay a slanted roof, which covered the outside toilet. If I could throw the contents of the jug out of the window, the snow would wash it away, If I could lean out far enough and fill my shoe with snow, I could wash the jug and also myself. The plan worked, or so I thought.

Grace did not arrive home until after dark, I was sure that the snow would do its duty in the night. But to my horror, the mess was still there the following morning. Later that day Grace came into the bedroom, carrying a yard brush. "That young plumber's lad has been throwing snowballs filled with sand on my roof. Just wait until I see his dad, I'll give him a piece of my mind." Grace pulled up the casement window, my heart began to thud, I was absolutely petrified. I cringed into the corner of my bed fully knowing what was to come. Grace began to shout. "What the hell," she gasped. "It's you isn't it you dirty pig, I'll kill you." I tried to explain my predicament in between blows, but she wasn't about to listen. I was beaten so badly, that evening I couldn't walk, my whole body felt like one giant bruise. My dad returned home from the pub,

Grace must have reported me to him, because he came into my room, took off his heavy leather belt and beat me soundly. This was the only time that I can recall my father hitting me in any real capacity, previously it had just been an odd cuff around the ear.

I fell into an exhausted sleep, weary from pain and crying. I now felt really sorry for myself, I was almost sure that Grace would eventually kill me. She hated me and I hated her. Such a strong feeling for an eleven year old girl to have to feel. I had often thought that I had hated people like Ma Mather, but I now experienced the true meaning of hate. It was a feeling that came from deep in my stomach that no child should ever have the necessity to feel.

During that night something stirred me from my sleep. It was a low whispering in my ear. "Your mother is a lunatic, she is mad, just like you, she is in the city asylum. You are going mad like her, it can be seen in your eyes. You will be locked away for the rest of your life."

I tried to focus my swollen bruised eyes. The room was dark, but I could just make out Grace's spiteful face in the dark, close to mine. She put her hand over my mouth preventing me from screaming and continued with her threats. Punching me in the stomach as she did so, completely winding me. I struggled begging her to stop; to leave me alone, to let me sleep. That it wasn't my fault that my mother was a loony, but Grace still persisted in tormenting me.

After that night I was often awoken in the same manner, eventually I expected and anticipated her threats. I began to feel that it was she who was mad, not me.

The following day was a Saturday, there was no way that I could go and serve in Miss Bird's shop, I looked as though I had been in a street accident. Grace called round to tell Miss Bird that I had caught a chill. For the first time that I can remember, I wanted to stay in bed, because I felt so ill, and could barely walk. Grace had other ideas though. She forced me to hobble down the stairs, dragging my one sheet and pillow case with me. She opened the back door, which led into the yard. The snow was still laying heavily on the ground. There standing in the middle of the yard was a white enamel bucket. "Kneel down there," Grace ordered. "Get your sheet and pillow case washed." The water was icy cold, the yard felt sore to my already bruised knees. Tears flowed down my cheeks as I knelt there, begging god to let me die. I was cold, bruised and Grace assured me that I was going to go mad. There was nothing else left to live for. After roughly an hour, Grace opened the back door and threw my school blouse and pants out. "Here wash these while you are at it," she sneered. She could see my small body was shivering with the cold, as my scanty nightdress clung to my pathetically thin body, but she was not going to relent, she felt no compassion. She gave me one of her evil I've won looks, then disappeared inside the warm house and closed the door. I was out there for over two hours, I had chilblains on my fingers and toes. The cast had now been set, this was the way that I carried out my laundry every week. I was also made to bathe myself in the same manner, for months no hot water touched my body. It was nothing short of a miracle that I never became ill.

CHAPTER ELEVEN

Spring term began, never had I been so pleased to return to school to get away from the dreadful clutches of Grace. My face still looked a mess. Grace had issued me with a set of instructions. "Tell your teachers that you fell off a bike if they ask." Which I dutifully did. My teachers would never have guessed the truth, at school I was very happy and out going, in fact over boisterous, and often cheeky. Most of the time I chatted merrily away in class, much to the distraction of the other pupils and the teachers, although I was doing well academically. School was my only outlet to express myself and let off steam. I tried very hard both in lessons and sport. It was necessary for me to push myself to prove that I was someone, to prove that I was equal to my classmates, if not better. I had aspirations for my future far further reaching than Grace's expectations for me.

Although, the impending prediction of my forthcoming madness hung over me like a cloud. Often, I would stare into the cloakroom mirror, trying to establish whether my eyes looked peculiar. Not being able to bear the suspense any longer, I approached my favourite teacher, Miss Wright. "Please, Miss," I asked. "Is there something wrong with my eyes? Are they different to anyone else's?" Humouring me, she stared deep into my eyes. "No Pearl, they are just a pretty blue, now get back to your lessons." So Grace had told me a malicious lie, I wasn't going to go mad after all.

Only one week into the Spring Term I tripped over in the playground, tearing the sole from the front of my shoe. My immediate reaction was, 'that's another good thrashing.' In fact I was so used to being thrashed that every time Grace passed near me, I would put my arm over my face to protect myself, flinching as I did so.

Although David was now well again, I was still not allowed to go home straight from school. David was a sickly child, who needed lots of attention. Grace was not aware that I went back to Pam's house, she was under the illusion that I stayed in school doing extra activities. "Won't do you any good all this learning," she would say, "It's the loony bin for you, just like your mother." Then she would gurgle with one of her evil laughs.

After school, I limped over to Pam, we were in different forms now. "Are you coming home?" she enquired.

"Yes please, perhaps your dad will fix my shoe for me." We laughed all the way home, at the exaggerated antics I was performing with the sole of my shoe. On arrival at Pam's house her dad was decorating the front room, he was carefully painting the panelling along the wall with brown paint. "Dad can you mend Pearl's shoe please, she can hardly walk?" He glued the sole onto the upper for me, and whilst waiting for it to dry we ate dripping sandwiches. When it was time for me to leave I slid my foot back into the shoe, thanked Mr Clarbour and made my way out through the front room.

I slipped, kicked the open paint tin, and the pa
splashed out all over the new decorating. Mr Clarbo
was livid and I was very upset. The Clarbours had
been very good to me, now I'd spoilt things. I walked
home, the paint affair weighing very heavily on my mind,
wondering if Pam would still be friends with me. By
the time I reached home, my sole was again hanging
off. "What's wrong with your shoe?" eagle eyed Grace
enquired. Sullenly I explained to her. I had far more
impending matters to think about, what with Pam and
all, the shoe was now the least of my worries. I lifted
my arm to protect my face, but Grace did not hit me.

The following day I could not go to school because
I didn't have any shoes to wear. Grace came upstairs,
measured my feet with a ruler, tied my door and left
the house. After about an hour the old familiar feeling
in my stomach began. The rumblings were really loud.
Trying in vain to control myself I paced the room, but
it was no good, nature was going to be unkind to me
again. What could I do? I dared not use the jug again,
the snow had now cleared, there would be nothing to
wash the jug with. Time was now running out, there
was only one consideration left. Previously when I
had been cleaning my room I had noted a broken
floorboard at the back of the bed, just under the
tattered linoleum. Swiftly I pulled out the bed and lifted
the floorboard, crouching in the corner I allowed nature
to take its course. This happened a further three times
that day. I opened the bedroom window, then sat there
shivering, hoping against hope that my bedroom would
not smell.

Grace arrived home, untied the bedroom door, and bade me to go downstairs. I flew past her straight outside to the toilet, where I cleaned myself with water from the toilet pan and dried myself with the newspaper, which I'd torn and threaded the day previous. Hopefully I had now covered all of my tracks and Grace would never find out about my accident. "Are you going to stay out there all day?" shouted Grace. "I have something for you." Intrigued, I raced back into the house, where a brown paper parcel was shoved under my nose. Ripping off the paper, I stared at the contents in astonishment. There in my hands were the ugliest, heaviest pair of black shoes I had ever seen. The soles were thick and bore a similarity to clogs. Blakies, a type of metal stud, had been hammered in the sole. "Do you like your new school shoes, Pearl?" Grace enquired Menacingly.

"Yes thank you," was my reply. I dare not tell her how ugly I thought they were, I had only just healed from my previous beating, I wasn't about to take another. Grace must have scoured the whole of Leicester to have found such an ugly pair of shoes. I could almost see the elation on her face when she came upon them.

What was I going to tell the girls at school, they would take the 'Mickey' out of me unmercifully. That night in bed I thought deeply, at last I came up with a plan of action. I would tell them that I was going to be a famous dancer when I left school, and that I needed to practice in this type of shoes, that they needed to be heavy to strengthen my legs.

The shoes clipped and clopped all the way down the street, I sounded like a cart horse out on his coal delivery round. When I entered the school, the shoes sounded so different on the hollow floor. I quite liked the sound and danced all around the school, clip clopping away. This annoyed the teachers intensely and it wasn't long before they made me change into my plimsolls, adding that if I wished to use my energies in such a way then I should attend the dance classes after school.

During playtime, Pam came to see me and told me that her dad had forgiven me, and that we were still friends, this was turning out to be a very good day after all.

After playtime we all filed into the religious knowledge class. The teacher began to tell us about the meaning of baptism, my ears pricked up. The teacher went on to say that the water poured over the small child's head was used to wash away sins of the parents. That's it, I've got it, I thought to myself using childlike logic, the priest did not pour enough water over my head to wash away my parent's sins, or else my dad was so evil fighting in the war and all that, I'd needed extra water. That must be why Ma and Grace hated me. I thought I now knew why my life was so difficult, and why Ma and Grace hated me. Why Uncle Charles had sent me away, this was the answer. I knew what I had to do. The rest of the afternoon dragged on, each minute feeling like an hour. I was impatient to get away.

At last, school was out, rushing over to Pam I explained that I would not be going home with her that afternoon, I had important business to attend to, I explained, although I could still greedily picture her mum's dripping sandwiches in my mind's eye. Still if my plan worked, perhaps I would get a big dinner tonight.

Cautiously I approached the church door, gently opened it, and silently slid inside. The church was empty. "Good," I said aloud. Approaching the altar I turned my eyes to Jesus on the large cross, which was hanging from the ceiling. "Please Jesus. Let this water work," I begged. I lifted the heavy wooden lid from the font with difficulty and gently placed the lid onto the floor, then climbed up onto the font and crawled inside. The bottom of the font was barely covered in water, but I thought that this would be enough. Standing on my head I dipped my brow and hair into the water and chanted, "I name me Pearl June, please take away the sins of my father." Clambering out I replaced the lid to its rightful place. There that should do it. I'm clean now, I'll soon be happy.

Just a few days later, I was laying on my bed playing with my Pug dolls, when a kind voice called, "Pearl come downstairs, I want to see you." Crikey! It's Grace speaking in a nice voice, I thought. The baptism had worked, I must have been full of sins. When I entered the living room, there sat a young man dressed in Naval Uniform, "this is my son William," Grace smiled sweetly. "He has come home on leave from the Navy, he has been away overseas." I liked William instantly, he had a gentle face that smiled a lot. The next few days were like heaven sent. William took me sailing in a canoe on the canal, he even let me wear his sailor's cap. We went for tea and cakes at the Boathouse cafe and walked along the river tow path. I was absolutely besotted. There and then I made up my mind that I would marry him when I grew up.

My happiness was short-lived, one night I heard raised voices, it was my dad and William arguing. Dad threw William out of the house that night. The next morning I paid with a ferocious beating. Grace ranted and screeched at me, "I have to have you in the house, you filthy little pig, but I can't have my own son, William. You'll pay for this." What the incident had to do with me I did not know. I loved William, why was she blaming me? When I could get out of the house, I sped to the church at top speed throwing open the large wooden door I ran to the altar shouting and screaming, "I hate you, I hate you God. Why did you only let the water last for a few days. I'm never coming into your house again, and I will never ever say my prayers." I was so angry I ran along the pews throwing the prayer books everywhere and tossing the hassocks into the air. Then I ran from the church sobbing uncontrollably and went away to hide.

The neighbourhood was fraught with gossip the following day, the church had been vandalised. Who would do such a thing to God's house? Inside I felt very ashamed about my outburst, but still blamed God for the water not working and keeping me happy.

Some days later I returned from Pam's house to find Grace in a violent rage. As soon as I entered the house, she began to hit me. "You dirty little bitch, I have found your hoard under the floorboards. I said that you were mad like your mother, now I have been proved right." She yanked me off my feet with my hair and dragged me into the yard, with me kicking and screaming all of the way. My head went down the toilet, the chain had not been pulled. "You like shit," she screamed, "you eat shit." The horrible mess entered my mouth. I was choking as she pushed the excreta further into my throat with her gloved hand. The old ladies from next door once again came to investigate the commotion. Grace was in too much of a frenzy to offer any explanations. She just carried on beating me and kicking me. After a short time a policeman arrived in our yard. "What's happening here then?" he asked as he took in the scene. Grace loosened her grip on me. She began to cry pitifully. "I just can't cope, Officer," she blubbered. "Just come and see what I have to put up with." We all went inside away from the prying eyes of the neighbours. "Now," said the policeman getting out his note book, "What's the story?" He listened intently to Grace's version of events, scribbling away in his notebook as she spoke. Turning to me he said, "Now young lady, what's your story." Eyes lowered to the ground I told him that Grace's story was true, and that I had nothing further to add. I was too afraid to tell my version for fear of reprisal once the policeman left. Grace took the policeman upstairs to view the evidence, he looked in amazement and proceeded to say, "The girl is obviously unbalanced, I'm aware that you must be frustrated, but beating her will not solve the problem. She needs psychiatric help, we will make arrangements for a Welfare Worker to visit you."

After the policeman had gone, I spent hours scrubbing out the bedroom, the linoleum was removed to leave the wooden floorboards exposed.

Grace did not hit me at all over the coming days, she was playing her cards close to her chest. She didn't want any new bruises appearing on my body, not with the anticipation of the social worker's arrival. All I could do was wonder what was in store for me, perhaps I would be sent back to the children's home.

CHAPTER TWELVE

It was Wednesday evening, the man from the Mutual was here. He gave Grace tickets that she could spend in the shops in the town. Every Wednesday she paid him five shillings. "Treating yourself are we Mrs Roberts?" he asked Grace.

"Something like that," she replied.

It was now Thursday morning. I arose at my usual early hour to prepare myself for school. I was bending over the bucket in the yard having my morning wash, when Grace called my name. "You can wash in the kitchen this morning, I've boiled you a kettle of nice hot water, your hair needs a good wash." Immediately I was on my guard, what was Grace up to, she never spoke to me in such a nice voice like that. I entered the kitchen covering my head with my arms as I passed by her, I was waiting for the slap or punch, but none came. She lowered my head into the white enamel bowl of hot water, I was expecting it to be scalding hot, it was not. She poured a sweet smelling shampoo onto my matted curly hair rubbing until my hair was squeaky clean. What was Grace up to, there had got to be a catch. I could not comprehend this kindness. When I was clean and dressed, Grace casually informed me that I would not be going to school that day or the day after that.

At nine o'clock we left the house, our first port of call was to the local men's barbers. The barber sat me in his chair, pumped it up to his eye level, commenting on what a mop of unruly hair I had. "Cut it short, and shape it a bit," said Grace. After much clipping, the barber showed me the end results in his hand mirror. What a transformation, the once tangled mass, now fell into soft curls around my face, the reflection that looked back at me was just like any normal little girl. On leaving the barbers we caught the bus into the city, where we headed for Lewis's Department Store.

Taking the escalator, we travelled three floors until we reached the children's department. First the underwear counter. Grace selected a vest and pants made from white embossed cotton, embellished with a small rosebud design. A far cry from my normal navy blue pantaloons with elasticated legs, one leg often slipped below my gym slip. The thought crossed my mind that the white pants wouldn't be any good to store apples in when I raided the apple trees at the end of my street. The navy blue pantaloons with the elastic legs could hold up to twelve apples, and still allow me to run like hell, when the owner spied me.

Next, onto the children's outerwear, where Grace chose a midnight blue dress, with white lace collar, and a coat in a darker shade of blue. We went into the dressing rooms where Grace assisted me in trying them on. My reflection in the mirror took me completely by surprise, in my mind I was transported back to the days when I lived with my Uncle Charles. Nostalgic memories came back to haunt me, I had to hold back the tears, thinking of those long sunny days playing with Charles and Eric.

The outfit was then complemented with white knee length socks, and dainty black shoes with a silver buckle. Why had Grace had this change of heart towards me? What was her motive? However, I just relished the moment before it was snatched away from me as was always the case.

Our next stop was Bruccianna's, where Grace bought me an ice-cream sundae, made with fresh strawberries and cream. It was impossible to remember when I had last had such a luxury. I guzzled it down almost wanting to lick the dish clean, of course this would have been impolite in such a posh place.

It was now time to make our way home, I was still waiting for Grace to drop a bombshell. I didn't have to wait long, barely were we back in the house, when she casually said, "Oh, by the way, I am taking you to see a psychiatrist tomorrow, he's a kind of doctor who asks you questions."

"Questions about what?" I enquired.

"About your home life here. If you dare say anything bad about me I'll beat your bloody head in. Just remember you have got to live here afterwards." Of course I knew what that meant, more beatings. My new appearance was all part of Grace's elaborate plan, the doctor would think that I was a cared for child in my nice new clothes and tidy hairstyle. It would put Grace in a good light.

I had made up my mind to tell the doctor my story about how cruel Grace was to me, I would not be part of her immoral plan. When the doctor knew the truth, Grace would be punished, I was sure that I could look after my dad, after all, he only ate cows' heels, pigs' trotters and mussels.

The night seemed long and burdensome. I tossed and turned wondering what the following day would bring. I arose at first light just as my father was leaving for work. "Make sure you tell the doctor the truth, Pearl," and he was gone. Of course Dad thought that Grace's stories were the truth.

We arrived at Belvoir House for my appointment with the psychiatrist, at nine thirty in the morning. I was dressed up in my purchases from the day before, if anything, Grace was dressed below her normal standard. The receptionist was very kind, she told Grace to wait then led me by the hand into a large pleasant room, where a table was set out with jig saws and puzzles. Once left alone I analysed the contents of the table, although feeling very tense and apprehensive, I made an attempt to fix a jigsaw puzzle. After fixing only a few pieces a lady entered the room. "Hello Pearl, I'm here to play some games with you, whilst your 'Aunt' is speaking with the doctor."

She talked with me for a while, asking me questions about my home and school life. Beginning to relax, I chattered away, and was quite happy to answer her questions. Picking up some blocks, the lady asked me to fix them into various holes, this seemed very easy, then other puzzles ensued. Some were easy some were not.

Right, the doctor will see you now, Pearl," the receptionist indicated as she reappeared. My stomach became knotted and the palms of my hands were damp as my fears returned. On entering the room, a tall well-groomed man approached me, placing his hand on my shoulder he introduced himself. "Hello, I'm Doctor James, you must be Pearl." He led me over to a chair. I was now gaining confidence, and began to relax, I told myself that he seemed like a nice man. Once I was seated he took a chair opposite me and stared directly into my eyes. "Now Pearl," he began, "are you happy living with Grace?" I lowered my eyes.

"No Sir," I mumbled.

"Do you miss your mother?" he asked.

"I don't remember her, Sir."

"Where would you like to live?"

"With my Uncle Charles Sir."

The endless questions went on and on, I tried to answer them all truthfully. Eventually Dr James asked, "Why did you put those stools in your bedroom Pearl?"

"I've got no stools in my bedroom," was my quick reply.

"Let me put it another way then, the poo you put under your floorboards," he said, leaning further across the desk, his face so close to mine that I could feel the warmth of his breath. I could no longer lower my eyes to the floor, but must look at him. Feeling terribly embarrassed, I slowly began to tell my story, the true version, his eyes were staring into mine the whole of the time. I edged further into my chair gripping the sides until my knuckles were white, as I continued, falteringly, the tears streamed down my face, at last I was unburdening myself of the horrors that I had experienced at the hands of Grace, burdens that were becoming so hard to shoulder. By the time I had finished my story, I was sobbing uncontrollably. Dr James gave me time to compose myself, then instructed me to tell him a fairy story, about what I thought would happen to my poo. "There is no fairy story to tell," I assured him, but he continued to coax me. At which I rambled off some idiocy to satisfy him, feeling rather stupid at having to tell such a story.

Story complete he called Grace into the room, gesturing her to sit beside me. Dr James went on to say, "I've reached my conclusion in this case. Given the mental history of Pearl's mother and the heredity factors, I consider Pearl to be severely unbalanced and a pathological liar. It is my opinion that she should be placed in a secure mental institution, for as long as it takes to heal her mind."

My jaw dropped open, this couldn't be true, Dr James had believed Grace instead of me. He came around the desk to shake hands with Grace and offer his condolences, "Do not reproach yourself, you have done everything possible to help the child, it must have been very difficult."

Anger raged inside of me, I threw my chair across the room, flung myself at the doctor, punching his chest and kicking his shins, this man had betrayed me. It was the first time I had told the truth to anyone with the exception of Pam, and he had not believed me, now he was going to lock me up in a lunatic asylum for the rest of my life. He caught hold of me and held me down to restrain me. "It would be better if you do not take Pearl home with you, please bring her belongings in this afternoon before four thirty." Still holding me in his grip, he beckoned Grace to leave. As she left the room, crocodile tears spilt down her face, she had got exactly what she had wanted, rid of me for good, in the cruellest possible fashion. Five shillings a week to the man at the Mutual was a cheap price to pay.

Alone with the doctor, I began to sob, "Please don't send me to that place." He simply ignored me and made a telephone call. The lady I had played games with earlier entered the room carrying a cold drink, which was offered to me along with a pill. The doctor said, "Take this Pearl, you will soon feel better." Before long I began to feel drowsy, and was soon nodding off in the chair. "Come along Pearl, you're going for a short drive." I was confronted by a uniformed man who gently carried me to a waiting car. It was just as though everything was happening in slow motion, it must have been the pill. Once in the car I was soon sound asleep. The next thing I knew, I was lying on a bed in a hospital room, another doctor in a white coat was leaning over me. I became aware of him speaking, his voice started to register in my mind it sounded as though it is coming from a long, long way away. "Hello Pearl, enjoy your little sleep," he was saying, "We have brought you to the Towers Hospital for the night, just to carry out a few tests on you." Little did I know that my mother was a patient in this same asylum. A coloured substance was then injected into my arm. I could not remember having ever been injected before, and became scared of the needle, at which the doctor became very impatient telling me, that I had better get used to them, as this would be the first of many in the years to come.

What appeared to be curlers hanging from a big stand, were placed over the whole area of my head. I was then told to make all sorts of faces to open and close my eyes and mouth, turn this way and that, whilst a screen at the side of me monitored the waves in my brain. The tests seemed to go on forever, I became fidgety, so I was strapped to the bed. Next I was taken to a small room, a nurse came with some food, after I had eaten, another pill was administered, I must have slept until morning.

When I awoke Doctor James was standing by my bed. "You seem a bit calmer now Pearl. I have decided to send you to a hospital in Surrey, that specialises in your type of illness."

"But I'm not ill sir," I replied.

"Let me be the judge of that," was all he said.

After breakfast, the same driver who had picked me up the previous day from Belvoir House, came to collect me. "Where are you taking me?" I asked. He told me that he was taking me to the London Road train station. He was a kindly man who chatted away to me, telling me that he had a little girl the same age as me. Although still a little lethargic from the drugs, I chatted back.

On arrival at the station I was introduced to a lady in uniform. "I'm nurse Giles," she told me. "I'm to travel with you to Surrey. Grace has given me your belongings." I see that she has my dad's army case in one hand, and my beloved teddy Alfie in the other.

"Alfie!" I squealed, grabbing him. I hadn't seen him since going to live with my dad. "Grace thought you would like to have him," added nurse Giles. That was the only time I could recall Grace showing any humanity towards me.

CHAPTER THIRTEEN

The train pulled into platform two, steam belching from its funnel into the early morning air, like a genie being released from its lamp. A great screeching of metal as the brakes brought the huge engine to a standstill. Carriage doors were thrown open, as the inbound commuters alighted. The awaiting outbound passengers surged forward all scrambling to board the train at once, each with the same intention, to capture the best seat. Nurse Giles grabbed my hand, joining the bustle dragging me along. We managed to secure a window seat and settled ourselves down on the plush, red velvet seats. Two pompous looking gentlemen in pin striped suits joined us in our compartment, and immediately vanished behind large newspapers. They were followed by two ladies of ample proportions who could have been going on a day's shopping spree to London. Within minutes they were knitting away contentedly.

This should have been an exciting day, being the first time that I had travelled by train, but it was impossible for me to gather together any enthusiasm. As the train shunted its way out of the station, I looked out of the carriage window and could suddenly feel panic rising in my throat, I was leaving friends like Pam, my school which I so much loved, Miss Bird's shop, and so many small things. It was like a firework going off in my mind, as the reality of the present situation hit me. Here I was, Pearl June Roberts, aged eleven and three-quarters, on my way to a lunatic asylum, far away from home, possibly for the rest of my life. I wanted to scream, "Please not me, take me home, take me back to The Cottage Homes, not to the asylum. I'm not mad." Was God punishing me for debasing his church during my terrible tantrum? Nurse Giles took my small hand in hers as she noticed the tears staining my cheeks, she could feel my scrawny body shaking with emotion. "It will be alright Pearl," she ventured as she squeezed my hand tightly, knowing full well that it wouldn't be. The compassion shone in her eyes as she spoke to me. This couldn't have been one of her easiest days. Looking into her eyes I told her beseechingly that my story, not Grace's, had been true. The recognition in her eyes told me that she believed me, but there was nothing she could do, she was just a messenger and not my persecutor.

Our travelling companions eyed us suspiciously, they must have contemplated on what a uniformed woman and a small girl in tears were doing travelling on an early morning train to London. One of the ample sized ladies rummaged in her knitting pack, pulled out a chocolate bar and offered it to me which I gratefully accepted with a watery smile and muffled words of thanks.

The train picked up speed as we reached the open countryside. I stared out of the window, at the cows standing idly in the fields lifting their heads in a transient manner, normally this would have captured my interest, but not today. The rhythm of the wheels on the track seemed to be in tune with my thoughts, as we trundled along, almost mocking me, as my very being reached the depth of despair. Nurse Giles explained to me that on arrival, she would hand me over to a man named Sam Sloane, that she must immediately catch the train back to Leicester.

The train pulled into St. Pancras station. Hurriedly leaving the train, we dashed along the busy platform towards a large clock, weaving amidst the busy sea of people. A fat man emerged from the crowd, waving a placard with 'St. Cuthberts' emblazoned across it. Nurse Giles said, "Ha, that must be Sam Sloane." To the man she said, "This is Pearl Roberts, your charge." He signed the form which she handed to him. "Must be off now to catch my train. Best of luck Pearl," and she was gone.

Sam led me by the hand to a waiting car, which was to be driven by a man in a navy uniform. This was the last leg of my journey to my dreaded new life.

CHAPTER FOURTEEN

As the car came to a halt, I caught the first sight of my 'New Home'. If it wasn't for the implications of the place, I would think it was quite pleasant. The building was set within nice gardens, with neatly kept lawns, close to the Epsom Downs. The air was fresh and quite warm, yet the place seemed isolated. As we approached the main door, I hugged Alfie tightly to me, he was the only thing that was familiar to me now. Sam rang the bell, I panicked, turned and began to run. Catching me by the collar, he said, "Not so fast young lady, you are going in here whether you like it or not." Holding me firmly by the arm he frog marched me into the building. "You've got a handful here, I don't envy the nurses on ward six," he stated to the porter who was sitting behind a large desk. "They'll soon break her spirit, she'll soon be like all the rest of the patients," he replied. I didn't fully understand what his meaning was, but I vowed there and then, that I would get out of this place. Sometime! Somehow!

A nurse appeared from behind a closed door, and bade me to follow her. We walked in silence along a desolate corridor until we reached a large Victorian bathroom. "Strip and bathe yourself, put this dress on when you have finished." I stood there, hoping that she was going to leave the room, I was not too keen on standing naked in front of her.

"Come along, chop, chop, we have not got all day."

"Can I bathe alone please?" I asked.

"No, sorry that's against the rules, just get cracking." I stripped and climbed into the oversized bath. "Where have you got those bruises from?" she observed. She was the first person to comment on them. "My Aunt Grace made them."

The nurse replied, "Well I suppose you deserved them." If I was looking for sympathy I certainly was not going to get it. I slipped into the dress that was made from blue serge material, the dress hung in all of the wrong places, it was far too big for me. I looked even thinner and scrawnier than I had done before. "We will take it to the tailors tomorrow, for alterations. We don't get many kids in this place," the nurse said as she eyed me critically. "Right! Let us get you to your ward." Whilst we were walking through the building, I noticed that the nurse unlocked each door which we came to, and locked it again after entry. "Why are you locking and unlocking all the doors?" I enquired.

"For security," was the answer. My childish wisdom told me, that she was afraid of robbers breaking in.

Eventually we reached the ward that I was going to live on. The nurse knocked on the door, and after a rattling of keys from the inside another nurse opened up with caution. I stepped inside. Nothing could have prepared me for the sight that met my eyes. I took in the whole spectrum in one glance.

The room was large, there were leather armchairs set out around the perimeter of the room. Each chair, with the exception of a few, was occupied by a woman, the patients varied greatly in age. Some just stared into space, others rocked back and forth, others were making strange sounds, whilst others sat soaked in their own urine. A small girl of about my age lay on a rug in the centre of the room nursing a doll. The smell of urine was sickening, the whole atmosphere was oppressive. I turned and ran towards the door, which I had just entered. I began to tug at the handle, but it would not budge. I began to scream, kicking and hammering on the door, with every ounce of energy that I possessed. "Let me out, Let me out," I shouted. "I'm not staying in this place, with these people." I became hysterical, throwing myself against the door. It took two nurses to restrain me. They tried to pull me back from the door by pushing me up against a wall. They held me in that position until a doctor arrived. "What's all this shouting about? We cannot tolerate such awful behaviour."

"I want to go home," I sobbed and continued to struggle and kick. The doctor placed his hand across my mouth to stop me from shouting. I bit into the side of his hand, the bite had drawn blood. "Why you little vixen you, for this you will pay dearly."

The two nurses and the doctor dragged me through the ward. I was screaming, shouting and struggling all the way. We came to a small room with no windows, just a sliding peep hole in the door. They roughly pushed me inside, stripped me of all my clothes until I stood there nude, then proceeded to dress me in a stiff jacket. They manoeuvred my arms inside of the sleeves, then they tied the sleeves around the back of me. I cannot move. After only two hours in the hospital, I was in a padded cell dressed in a straight-jacket. "See if this cools your temper, Roberts," the doctor chided. "We will not tolerate your tantrums here."

I screamed and struggled until I became exhausted. I felt like a wild animal trapped in a cage, my head felt as though it would explode with the frustration at not being able to move. In my struggle, I had fallen onto my back and was unable to sit up again. After some time, it became obvious to me that no-one was going to heed my screams. Logic took over and I silenced myself, apart from my sobs, which came from deep inside me, these I could not prevent. If I kept quiet the doctor would let me out, I reasoned with myself. I lay there filled with intrepid fear, my vivid imagination took over, all sorts of imaginings crossed my mind. What if they kept me like this forever and I really did go mad? I had to keep myself occupied, I looked around the cell and noticed that the whole room, from floor to ceiling, contained only cork. The cork was shaded with various colours. This was it, I thought, I would count all the interlaced pieces, just like I had counted the flowers in my bedroom at home. After a very long time, the doctor I had bitten came to take me out of the straight-jacket. I noticed that his hand was heavily bandaged. I felt guilty for hurting him.

"Here's your clothes, Pearl, get dressed. Let's hope that this spell in here has taught you a lesson. If not, then this will be your punishment, each time you are really bad, until you do learn."

As you can imagine, that wasn't to be the last time, which I would spend in the 'Bouncing Box', as the more rational patients called it. Within a few months, I got to know the cork tiles intimately. One would think that one experience in the bouncing box, would be sufficient to force anyone to curtail their temper in the future, but not me. I was far too stubborn and high spirited.

Once dressed, the doctor handed me over to one of the nurses. "Go to the day room until supper time," the nurse directed. After finding a seat that wasn't wet, I began to study my fellow inmates, it wasn't a pretty sight to behold. After a few moments, the other child resident shyly approached me. "Why are you in here?" she asked.

"For nothing, it's just that no-one likes me," I replied.

"My name is Pat and I am a pyromaniac," the girl said.

"What's one of those?" I asked.

"I like to light fires and play with matches." Pat seemed normal to me, just like Pam and my friends from my last school. We became great friends, it was a matter of Hobson's Choice, being the only two children in St. Cuthberts.

Pat suggested that she take me around the room to introduce me to some of the other people. I was not that keen really, just looking at some of them made me feel afraid. However, at the insistence of Pat, we began our rounds. First there was Nora, a very old lady, who was sucking the web of her hand between her thumb and index finger. She had nasty sores on her chin from the constant dribble of saliva. Ma would have died of fright if she saw the scabs on this face, I nostalgically snigger to myself. Next came Alice, her Lyle stockings hung around her ankles, her legs were covered in vicious open ulcers. We moved on to Jean, her stockings and dress were drenched with urine, she absolutely reeks. "Bugger off, you little sods," she said, as we attempted to speak with her. I took great delight after that to goad her into speaking, and each time I would give her the same response as she, by saying, "Bugger off yourself," then I would run away laughing. Pat continued the rounds. "That's Hattie in that chair, no good talking to her she never speaks," Pat said, pointing to a woman who simply stared into space as we passed by her. The next lady stood up, extended her hand in welcome, and in a cultured voice announced herself as, "Miss Steadly. What a shame, another child in this terrible place," she said emotionally. Then there was Flora, she shouted obscenities at everyone who passed her chair. Nancy was strapped into her chair, she stripped naked and ran around the room shouting that she was 'Queen Victoria'.

The list went on. Many more women, many with profound mental disabilities, some who had just experienced nervous breakdowns, inhabited the ward. It suddenly struck me with some force that Doctor James must have thought that I was as badly mentally sick as some of these people, for me to have even been considered to be sent to such a place. A shiver passed through my body, I began to ponder at what my chances were of getting out of this place. My earlier convictions on arrival, were shrinking rapidly.

The sound of a gong echoed round the room. Patients who had been staring fixedly on one spot, suddenly came to life, as if by magic. They began to rush, some with sticks, others with walking frames, with one aim, to get to the door at the opposite side of the room. "It's supper time," Pat explained. We joined the mad rush. The dining room was set out with tables which seated four. I was seated next to Nora, Miss Steadly, and a lady called Joyce. The meal began. The food was good. Nora was dribbling into her food, Joyce decided it was time to cough up phlegm into a spittle, which she carried with her. My appetite deserted me immediately. "Don't worry, you'll get used to it all," Miss Steadly confirmed. Although, at that moment that just didn't seem possible to me.

With supper over the mammoth task of getting patients to bed began. "Roberts, come with me," a nurse ordered. She led me into a huge dormitory which slept every patient on the ward. "We won't be sleeping you next to Pat, the pair of you will chat all night." My bed was situated in between two of the worst afflicted women. I was issued with a long white cotton night gown, again, this is not my size at all, being far too long. I look like 'Wee Willie Winkie', ready for his rounds.

The medicine trolley trundled up the ward, some patients were administered a foul smelling clear liquid, the odour lingered in the air. The nurse told me it was a drug called Paraldehyde, and wouldn't you just know it, my bed neighbours both received a dose. "You have tablets to take Pearl," said the nurse as she proffers a small medicine glass.

"Why?" I asked. "I'm not ill."

"You have bad anaemia, your blood needs building up, it's because you have been a naughty girl and have not eaten your dinners." Opportunity would have been a great thing, I reflected. "You also need a small pill to help your brain to mend," the nurse continued.

"There's nothing wrong with my brain," I rudely retorted. The second pill has made me feel very sleepy, but still I fought to keep awake by sitting bolt upright. My bed neighbours worried me immensely. Visionary, I felt that they may strangle me in the night. An eleven year old child's imagination is second to none.

The night was a troubled one, an overhead light in the centre of the ward shone persistently throughout. It kept the patients awake, they screamed and shouted and some pleaded to God to let them die. They were so hardened to their drugs, that they no longer worked so efficiently. The whole affair was like being in the middle of an nightmare, from which it was incapable of waking up.

The next morning arrived along with the tablet trolley. My pills were again administered to me. Within minutes I felt lethargic and disinterested in what was happening around me. I no longer felt angry or afraid, I wanted to lie on the floor and rest. I felt as though I was seeing through a fog. Much of my day was spent in this manner. I submitted to every order. I tried to establish some organisation in my mind, I gathered that the pill was the cause of my present dilemma. As I was thinking this through in my mind, I told myself that I would hide them and flush them down the toilet at a convenient time.

By tea time some of my spirit had returned, and I sat and read a book. There were no other activities to pursue. Whilst I was eating my tea the nurse told me that the psychiatrist wished to see me. He was a severe man who asked me lots of questions, some about sex. I did not know what he was talking about, for I had no knowledge of the subject. "I don't like the pills that you give to me," I told him.

"If you cease throwing tantrums, we will stop them. Each time you are out of control, you will either be administered a pill, or put into the padded cell. The choice is yours, behave or pay the consequences." It was obvious that I was going to be in a no win situation in this place. The ward housed a small schoolroom, Pat and I attended two mornings a week, each morning was for a four hour session. We would read a little, do elementary maths, and a little geography. The rest of the time was engaged in arts and crafts. The teacher's name was Mr Posnett, he was an elderly man, who must have been at the back end of his teaching career.

One day I asked him, "Why do I have to do such easy work?"

The reply was, "This is the curriculum which the authorities have set for you, I must abide by it. Doctor James, has assessed you as below average intelligence." This seemed impossible to me, after all hadn't I been in the Alpha Stream, at Sir Jonathan North School? If I was below average intelligence, the children in the lower forms at my school must have been imbeciles. Mr Posnett said that he could not comment. "I'm here to teach, nothing more."

In the craft class I made some tea cosies and oven gloves made from felt. I crafted one cosy into the shape of a cottage, with windows, a door even a chimney, the bottom I embroidered with cottage garden flowers. "Now your projects are complete, you may send them to your relatives for gifts," Mr Posnett told us.

No matter how hard I try, I cannot comprehend why I sent my cottage to Grace, the woman who had been the instigator into getting me into that hell hole. My memories of the time spent there are so vivid, I know that I shall never forget them...

It's a nice warm day today, some of us are allowed to walk out into a walled garden, there are no flowers, but lots of trees, shrubs and lawn. There is a sturdy gate at the end of the garden, this is padlocked with a heavy lock, and chain. There is no hope of getting out through this gate. I run and run, round and round the garden, I feel the fresh air in my face, the nauseous smell of the hospital behind me, I think that this is how an animal must feel, when it is first let out of its cage.

I've exhausted myself and sit on the grass, Miss Steadly comes to sit beside me. "Enjoying the fresh air? So young to be cooped up in a place like this," she says with much compassion. I learn that she is a Head Mistress at a girls school, and has experienced a nervous breakdown. "I thought you weren't nutty like the others," I tell her. She smiles and affectionately ruffles my hair.

Each time we were let out into the garden after that, I would walk with her, she taught me the names of the shrubs, trees and the birds. She taught me about the stars and astronomy, she covered all manner of subjects, we discussed and she allowed me to argue. It was like having a private tutor. I like to feel in some small way, that I was therapeutic to her, and that our unusual friendship aided in her recovery. When she recovered and left the hospital I was distraught, I wept for days, we had become such good friends. "I cannot visit you in this place Pearl, it has too many unhappy memories for me, but trust me, you are not mentally sick and one day you will take your rightful place in the outside world," she told me on our last walk. Often when I felt distressed I would remember her words.

She often wrote to me and sent me comics. One day there was a competition in one of the comics, I filled in the entry form and sent it off. Two weeks later a ten shilling postal order arrived, I had won a runners up prize. Thereafter, I entered every competition I saw, and on each occasion I won something. I now suspect that it was the address that caused the judicatories to take pity on me.

Once I had settled into the hospital, the nurses started to befriend me. Nurse Jenny became my favourite, she was young and pretty and would tell me stories about London, she would bring photographs of her at dances and the like for me to look at. I would feel envy and wonder whether I would ever go to a dance hall. Sometimes when she wasn't busy she would teach me dance steps.

Some of the patients received insulin treatment, whereby they would be put to sleep for many days, then injected with insulin. They would be fed by tube, through the nose, and mucous would be drawn from their throat into kidney bowls. They would just lay there in a comatose state, sweating profusely. When the treatment was complete they would be dragged along the floor, by their night wear and thrown into a cold bath, to revive them. Often they would come round and have completely different personalities, within day they would be discharged from St. Cuthberts.

One such lady never ate, she hoarded all her food in a locker, it was crammed full of mouldy food. After receiving the insulin treatment, she didn't know how the food had got there and was appalled at the state of the locker, she was discharged the following day.

A plan evolved in my mind. That's it, I thought, if I can get to have this treatment the doctors will discharge me. That afternoon, I climbed onto my bed and began to moan, I purposely peed on the eiderdown, and forced slobber to dribble from my mouth. "Get up Pearl, what do you think you are doing?" the staff nurse wanted to know. I didn't give her an answer but began to roll my eyes and let my tongue slip loosely from my mouth. She dragged me from the bed and shook me, "You will change that bed yourself," she said. All I got for my troubles was an hour in the bouncing box.

"You'll earn your keep, after yesterday's episode," I was told. The chores which I was given were most disagreeable. The most hated one was emptying and

117

washing the kidney bowls which were full with mucous from the insulin patients. Each time, I would stand in the sluice retching at the very sight of it.

After a few weeks I lost my fear of the other patients and was able to stand up to them and defend myself, after all, there had been plenty of room for practice in my life before St. Cuthberts. Sleep now came easily to me, within minutes of my head touching the pillow I would be in the land of nod. One night I was aroused from a deep sleep. I felt someone in the small single bed beside me, the smell of urine and paraldehyde was overpowering, I felt hot breath on my face, hands were fondling my body. I felt a weight climb on top of me, hands began to explore my private parts, trying to thrust something inside me. I was struggling with all my might, I realised that this person was Jean. I managed to get free and ran screaming up the ward. The night nurse came rushing out of her office. "Whatever is wrong Pearl?" she asked . I was shaking, she took me into her office and I explained. Nurse ran down the ward, but Jean was back in her bed feigning sleep. "Get back to bed Pearl, we will deal with this in the morning," instructed Nurse. Sleep did not come easy to me for the rest of that night.

Barely had I finished Breakfast, when Nurse Jenny shouted down the ward, "Doctor's here to see you Pearl."

His first words to me were, "I am most annoyed with you about last night's episode."

"Why are you annoyed with me Doctor? The disturbance wasn't my fault."

"No it never is Pearl, I really thought you had got out of the habit of telling lies. Poor Jean is far too sick to defend her name." I tried to argue, but he silenced me with a wave of his hand. That night my bed was moved to another part of the ward, the nurses were obviously taking no chances.

After that incident my meetings with the doctor became more frequent and more intense. He said I told lies, I said I told the truth. The meetings became confrontations, nothing constructive came out of them at all.

To this day I have a phobia about meetings, which has possibly hindered my career. The memories of my time at St. Cuthberts continued to flow...

School has just finished, I wander into the day room to see who I can spitefully tease today. Muriel, a new patient of just a few days, is perched on a radiator, I notice she has forgotten to put on her pants. What I see next shocks me beyond belief. "Nurse, Nurse come quick, Muriel has cut herself in her unmentionables." Muriel was quickly shooed away, I was taken to the nurse's office, where she carefully explained menstruation and childbirth to me. She said it was a private and personal thing and that Muriel was very naughty. That was my shocking introduction to the 'birds and the bees'.

CHAPTER FIFTEEN

Oh dear, my throat is so sore again this morning, my temperature is high, I can hardly swallow. The medical doctor is coming to visit me this morning, this is the third really nasty throat infection I've had in as many months, this one is making me feel so weak, that I am confined to bed.

The Doctor has been, he has put me in isolation, I don't like this room, this is where the old ladies are put when they are ill, they sometimes die, and being imaginative I can almost feel their souls floating around the room. My temperature must be brought back to normal, then I am going to be admitted to Guys Hospital, to have my tonsils removed. My visitors today are constant, the old dears are worried about me being in the critically ill room. I manage to croak that I only have a poorly throat.

I arrive at Guys, accompanied by a nurse and driver from St. Cuthberts. They take one arm each, firmly holding me to make sure that I don't do a runner. We report to reception, "Patient from St. Cathberts," announced the driver, immediately two porters appear.

"Right we'll take her." They take me to a side room adjacent to the main Medical ward, where a nurse is immediately assigned to me. "I must get you straight into bed," she announces. Once in bed she closes the door and stands guard over me. "Why are you guarding me?" I wanted to know.

"All patients from St. Cuthberts are treated in this way," was her reply. This made me feel like a criminal, she probably thought I was a raving lunatic and was going to attack someone at any moment. When the consultant arrived, he looked surprised. "You are only a child," he said. He sat on my bed, took my hand and explained the operation to me. I asked him questions, and he willingly answered. "When the operation has been performed, I want her transferred to the Children's ward," he instructed the nurse.

"But Sir," stammered the nurse.

"No buts, just do it," he said.

When I came round from the anaesthetic, I was in a bed in the Children's ward, just as the doctor had requested. My diet consisted of jelly and ice-cream. Visiting times were difficult for me, the other children's parents visited them, they got lots of hugs, kisses and presents. Their parents stared at me curiously, no doubt wondering why my visitor's chair was always empty.

That stay in hospital made me realise how different I was from other children, I felt totally isolated and alone, and longed for someone to visit me and hug me. On the fourth day of my stay, the double doors opened to let in the evening visitors. A man in a tweed jacket approached my bed. "I thought you would like a visitor," he said, handing me a parcel wrapped in pretty paper. I realised he was the Consultant who had performed my operation.

"Open your gift," he said. Excitedly I tore off the paper to reveal a beautiful book of Children's Stories, containing lots of colourful pictures. "Thank you so much, the book is lovely," I said, it was difficult to hold back the tears. The bell rang, announcing that visiting time was over. The Consultant leaned over and gently kissed me on the forehead. I was only twelve and could not remember the last time that anyone had kissed me.

Soon it was time to go back to St. Cuthberts. My throat was healing well, the soreness had all gone. The driver and nurse came to collect me, the Guy's nurses all waved me off, with sadness in their eyes, they knew where I was to return to.

I turned to take one last look and wished that my recovery had taken forever.

CHAPTER SIXTEEN

When I enter the ward on my return to St. Cuthberts all hell breaks loose, the old ladies rattle their chairs, and rock even harder, Jean pees herself with excitement, they are all so pleased to see me return. What an odd welcoming committee, it makes me feel quite depressed after spending a few days in the 'normal' world. The oppressive odour appears to smell even stronger than before. To my disappointment, Pat has been discharged, I am now the only child on the ward and do not look forward to the prospect, it's certainly going to be lonely. I look around the day room and the very thought of being the only child makes me feel totally isolated, will my mind eventually turn to be like these poor women sitting idly around in chairs, my stomach starts to turn summersaults, now I am very afraid, running from the room I lie on my bed and sob and sob, there is no-one who can console me. I think I would sooner be dead than spend any more time in this place. My heart screamed for someone to believe that my mind was normal, never in all of my life had I prayed so hard for something.

A few days later I entered the day room, Mr Posnett my teacher arrived. Switching on the radio, he commanded everyone to be silent. The radio blared out, "The King is dead, he died peacefully in his sleep." The announcement was followed by much wailing and sobbing from the patients, the nurses cried silently. Not fully understanding what was happening I thought I had better cry too, and struggled to shed a few tears. King George VI had died. The patients were in an agitated state for the rest of the day. Given their mental state, it was incredible to think that these women could reach such depth of mourning.

Once the mourning of the King was over, the whole country began to celebrate the Coronation of Queen Elizabeth II. The people of Britain embraced the pomp and ceremony, street parties where held throughout the nation. Me, I had a special tea in the walled garden, and was presented with a Union Jack flag.

Time passed by, then one morning I was called in for my meeting with the psychiatrist. I sullenly entered the room ready for my 'confrontation', and stopped dead in my tracks. Sitting behind the desk was a lot younger, more handsome man, than my normal doctor.

"Hello, I'm Doctor Mansfield, your new psychiatrist. I shall be working with you twice a week." He has laughing eyes and a carefree manner. "I have read your case notes and want to try something a little different." He went on to explain, "We will take a walk on the Epsom Downs, whenever the weather permits, you will tell me a little of your story each time." Normally I sat slumped in the chair, eyes staring fixedly on the floor, swinging my legs nonchalantly. That day this doctor had my full attention, I was immediately seduced by his charm. We chatted some more and made arrangements to meet on Friday, dressed in outdoor clothes. The walks became the highlight of my life, I thought that I was a little in love with Doctor

Mansfield. My first school girl's crush I suppose. I talked and talked and was neither apprehensive nor embarrassed as with the previous doctor.

After a few weeks of therapy and in-depth conversation, it became apparent that Grace had blackened my character far more than I had previously realised. It was too incredible for me to imagine, but she had told Doctor James at Belvoir House, that I had loitered outside of the men's toilets on the recreational ground, trying to procure men for sexual purposes, that I had been doing this since I was ten years of age. She had also insisted that I had known carnal knowledge of a man. I remember she used to say this to me when ranting, but had no idea what she was talking about. I had no idea what sexual purposes were, sex to me was a matter of gender, meaning that I knew that there was a man and a woman in the human species. I was completely sexually naive. I had celebrated my thirteenth birthday the previous week, and had never experienced an intimate kiss. Everything to do with the opposite sex was a complete enigma to me.

Grace had told further stories of me accosting men in the streets, for a similar purpose. Granted, myself and the rest of the girls in my form at school had stopped men in the streets, but it had been for a completely different reason. American G.I.s frequented the district where I lived. We would pass them by and say, "Got any gum, chum," and they would throw packets of spearmint chewing gum to us. I would chew mine with relish, and each time I procured another packet, I would add it to the gum that I already had in my mouth. My pals and I would have a contest to see who could chew the largest ball of gum. Each evening when I returned home from Pam's, I would stick the gum under the sill of the outside front window, then retrieve it in the morning and merrily go off to school chewing the same gum. During lessons I would stick the gum under my desk, as our form teacher would not allow us to chew in class. My ball of gum was always the largest, it was impossible to close my mouth whilst chewing, my pals never twigged why mine was so big.

It was inconceivable that the psychiatrist had believed Grace, given that sex in the forties was a taboo subject, there was no way children could have gained sexual knowledge, especially the sort of which I was accused. The doctor must have thought that I had been born a pervert.

Drastic changes began to take place in my life at St. Cathberts after my sessions with Doctor Mansfield. Firstly, I was given three sets of clothes which were far more suited to my age group, and I was allowed to wear them daily. This boosted my morale in a big way, they made me feel less institutionalised. Next, I was told that I would never again be put into the padded cell, which was a great relief.

After some weeks I had exhausted my story, Doctor Mansfield looked me directly in the eyes. "Pearl Roberts, I have finished my assessment of you."

"And?" was all I could utter, hardly daring to breathe, it was unlikely he had believed me, no-one ever had done so in the past, why should he be any different?

"I think you have been telling me the truth, during your sessions with me. There has been a terrible miscarriage of judgement. You should not really be in this place, we will see if anyone else will take you. Do not get your hopes up, I cannot promise you anything definite." My head began to spin. The whole of my body became hot, I felt as though a volcano was about to erupt inside me. He believed me, someone believed me at last. It was as though the whole of my childhood was flooding before me in one foul swoop. All the fears, frustrations, anger, and often the terror, the great need to be loved, were all forces fighting for first place in a torrent of emotion. I began to shake uncontrollably, next came the sobs, sobs which seemed to come from the depths of my soul.

Ten years had been a long time for a child to live without love. Without an affectionate glance, a good night cuddle, the protection of a guiding hand, the look of pride from a parent on parent's evening at school, knowing that you had excelled in one area or another. These were the things that mattered and I had experienced none of them throughout my childhood. The great injustice I felt that throughout those ten years everyone had assumed that every word that I had uttered had been a lie, that every naughty deed I committed had been assumed to be premeditated instead of simply being accepted as the spontaneity of childhood. As a child, these had been the hardest things to bare.

When Doctor Mansfield saw my awesome reaction, his eyes told me that he knew without a doubt, that he had backed the right horse. Once the initial trauma was over and I began to realise the implications of Doctor Mansfield's findings, I became overwhelmed at the prospect of getting out of that place. I so intoxicated Staff Nurse with my enthusiasm, that she agreed to find the addresses of all my relatives. She assumed that I just wanted to write and tell them all my good news, but she was wrong. I had hatched a plan in my mind to help Doctor Mansfield to place me. I wrote five letters, each reading very much the same. Four to aunts and uncles, and one to my Grandpa. They read, "Dear Grandpa, Uncle etc., The doctor now knows that I am not mad like my mum, I can come out of this place, if someone will take me in. Please can I stay with you, I will try to be very good and help you with your housework. Please let me know soon. Love as always Pearl."

I then passed the letters on to Nurse Jenny to post.

Every morning found me at the Staff Nurse's office, popping my head around the door I would enquire, "Any letters for me?"

She would answer, "Not today Pearl, try tomorrow."

After two weeks I was getting very disheartened, no further news had come from the doctor, there were no replies to my letters. Then one morning the nurse said, "Yes, you have a parcel today Pearl." Inside was a six inch sugar pink pig, with a blue ribbon tied around its neck, the parcel also contained a letter. "Dear Pearl, hope you enjoy this pig, but I am sorry I cannot take you in, I have never had children and I would not know how to handle you. Hope you get sorted. Love Aunt Emma" She was my father's sister who lived in London. Still, never mind I thought as I sat and ate the pig, there were still four more replies to come.

Some days later, Staff Nurse came rushing out of her office waving a letter, "For you Pearl at last!" she shouted. This time the letter was from Grandpa.

"Dear Pellard, Grandma has taken a turn for the worse. I must sell the shop. Your Uncle Charles has built a bungalow for us at Groby, so that we can live close by him. I cannot take on the extra responsibility of looking after you. You are in the best place. Yours Grandpa." The three remaining letters were never answered.

Doctor Mansfield called me into the office a few days later. "I am sorry Pearl, I cannot find anyone to take you. None of the children's homes will take a child from St. Cuthberts, but I will keep trying, I promise you."

My morale began to plummet. Although not bodily mature, I was beginning to show obvious signs of puberty, I would soon be a young woman, the childhood image that people so pitied would soon be lost forever, then the Mental Health system would swallow me up and I would be like the Alices and Jeans locked away in that infernal place for the rest of my life, too institutionalised to serve any real purpose in society.

Time was definitely running out, I began to pray to God even harder. "Please find someone to take me,"

I would almost beg, as I knelt to say my bedtime prayers, prayers that often felt so futile, but were part of the hospital discipline.

Life carried on much the same as usual at St. Cuthberts...

This scarf I'm knitting certainly takes some concentration, it looks more like a lace dishcloth because there are so many dropped stitches. Someone stands in my light, I look up with the intention of giving whoever it is a piece of my mind, and stop midstream, there stands William, dressed in his Naval Uniform.

"Hi ya, Pearl." The knitting drops to the floor, I throw myself at him, hugging him for all my worth, not wanting to let him go. He puts me at arms length, cups my face in his large hands and says, "Oh Pearl, my little Pearly, what are you doing in a place like this?" He looks around the room with complete disdain, the shock on his face is apparent. He tells me that he has been working overseas and that he is now stationed in Chatham. We talk and laugh for about two hours. When he gets up to go I cling to him. "Please take me with you." He explains that he lives in barracks, and that children cannot live there. William promises to visit me on a regular basis, whilst he is ashore.

Soon after William's visit, Doctor Mansfield wishes to see me again. "Pearl, I have some news for you. You are to leave St. Cathberts next Friday, William has convinced the authorities back in Leicester, that St. Cathberts is entirely the wrong place for you, therefore your father has agreed to take you back."

Trembling, I asked, "Is Grace still living with my dad?"

"Yes she is," he replied.

I just could not believe that I was being returned to my persecutor, the very root cause of my present difficulties.

"Listen carefully," Doctor Mansfield continued. "This is the only way to get you out of here. You will be given a permanent, fortnightly visiting supervision order. If thing's don't work out in your father's house, the Children's Home will be forced to take you, for your protection. We will refuse to have you back at St. Cathberts." I eyed him warily. "Embrace it Pearl, be brave, you will be fine, you have such pluck." Knowing that he still believed in me, I agreed to his plan.

Friday soon arrives, sleep evaded me last night, and today is my last day in this vile place. William arrives to take me to Leicester. It is time to say goodbye to the patients. In some bizarre sort of way, I have built up an affection towards these very odd, sad women. I eventually get to Jean. "Cheerio you bugger," I say.

"Bugger off, you little sod," the usual reply, this is all I have ever heard her utter, then she grabs my hand and clutches it tightly. To my amazement she says, "Be happy girl," just one tear rolls down her cheek. Although I have teased her unmercifully, mainly because of her attempted rape on me, I suddenly felt pity for her, the only time that she would leave this hospital was in a coffin. I placed Alfie, my teddy in her arms, "For you," I said. "Take care of him, Jean."

I then left the ward without looking back.

CHAPTER SEVENTEEN

The feeling of freedom as I walked through the doors of St. Cuthberts with William was something which I will never forget. I felt so exhilarated it almost took my breath away, how lucky I had been when I had been appointed my new doctor and how fortunate that William had visited. These two chances of fate had saved me from a lifetime of confinement and misery. If necessary, I would have run all the way to St. Pancras Station, I never ever wanted to go near Epsom again. If only I could have discarded all of my clothes, jumped into a hot bath, and soaked for days in order to wash the smell of the hospital from me.

St. Pancras was so noisy, I clutched hold of William's hand, the deafening noise was very frightening after the solitude of the hospital. We had a drink in the cafeteria, everything seemed so strange, seeing normal people in a normal place. I was relieved when our train was announced, we would at least have the privacy of the small compartment.

On the journey home, it became evident that William did not realise the reason that I had been institutionalised, or the involvement his mother had had in my confinement. My sixth sense told me to keep my own counsel. I tell him that I am too embarrassed to discuss my past predicament.

As we neared our destination, I began to feel very apprehensive. The thought of meeting Grace again was quite scary. What sort of reception would I get? Would she feel any remorse for her evil deeds? Did she really want me in the house again, after going to such great lengths to be rid of me previously? My biggest fear was that she had been accused by the authorities of lying about me. What would her reaction be?

My reception was much as I had expected, no red carpet treatment, just cold politeness from Grace and a insouciant attitude from my dad. William had a quick cup of tea and left. It was obvious that the rift between him and my dad still existed.

David had grown up and was now of school age. He broke the ice by coming over to me and saying, "Are you Pearl?" He didn't remember me, but it was apparent that he wanted us to be friends, at least it gave me someone to talk to at such an awkward moment.

The house had changed very little, with the exception of the yard, which had all been cleared up, probably because of David's illness. The plumbing rubble had all gone and had been replaced with slabs. The brick copper had been removed from the kitchen, and a small galvanised boiler stood in its place.

It was not long before my dad donned his best suit and made for the pub, this was the moment I was dreading, being left alone in the house with Grace. Although it was late summer, the evenings were still light. I think it is better if I get out of the way so decide to take a walk around the nearby streets. "Not so fast young lady, we need to talk." I froze, here we go again. "I don't know how you have managed to wrap William around your little finger, or fool the authorities into letting you come home, you may not have done the things which you were locked away for, but you have a madness in you all the same. It's in your blood, sooner or later it will manifest itself." This time I looked her straight in the eyes without wavering. "Neither you, nor anyone else, will ever get me in a place like St. Cuthberts again, I'd sooner die first. You can't hurt me now, I am seeing the Welfare every fortnight, if they see any bruises on me, you'll be for it." We continued to banter for some time, her knuckles were white with rage, but she dare not hit me. I turned away and went for my walk, the first time that I had walked freely for so long. However, my enjoyment was marred by my uncharitable thoughts of Grace, seeing her again had brought to the fore all the hatred of her which I had tried to bury. The wounds which she had inflicted on my mind were so deep it was as though a venom had been injected into my soul, just waiting to be released to strike its prey. The return to my father's household had got to be wrong for both Grace and myself. Although I was older, I was very vulnerable. I had built a wall around myself, it was possible that I now needed counselling to help me deal with life outside the hospital. The 'powers that be' had returned my liberty to me, but it was up to me to cope at thirteen and this was a very tall order. I just hoped that I would be strong enough to take Grace on again.

The Welfare decided not to send me back to Sir Jonathan North School, they felt that I would be a sitting target for ridicule from the other children who knew where I had been. My alternative was a school two miles away, in a different area. Although it was a lot further to walk, the consensus was that I would get a better chance there to get back into the normal swing of life.

No trips to the rag and bone yard this time round. The Welfare rigged me out with a whole new uniform, including all the necessary sports kit. This would be the first time ever that I attended school dressed the same as everyone else, and not looking like a scarecrow. Previously, I had always worn pants and vest for gym, which weren't always ultra clean either.

On my first morning I felt really smart, looking at myself in Grace's mirror I thought to myself confidently, this time I'm going to make it. It was impossible for the school to grade me, because of the time I had lost from my mainstream school, so the first morning was taken up with a number of tests. I had enough marks to place me in the middle grade. I have a lot of catching up to do to make Alpha again, but I would use all my determination to make it eventually.

The headmistress took me to my classroom, where she introduced me to my new form teacher. Thirty five pairs of eyes were upon me, but this time I was not bothered for I looked the same as they did. There was no way they could possibly know about my past. As I was shown to my desk some girls sniggered behind their hands, others eyed me suspiciously, I mistakenly thought that this was because I was a new girl. Come break-time, a bunch of girls sidled up to me and said,

"You've been in the nut house, haven't you, what was it like?" Grace had obviously made sure that I wasn't going to be allowed to forget the past. The pupils avoided me like the plague, except to call me 'nutter' or 'loony'. It came to the stage where I dared not answer questions in class, in case I gave the wrong answer and was ridiculed.

Grace would not allow me to wear a bra even though I was now developing.

One lunch-break, I was sitting alone in the playground reading, when a bunch of girls came along and started to throw stones at my feet, chanting, "Make the nutter's tits bounce." I saw red, I could not take anymore from these spiteful girls. The next thing I knew, I was laying into them, kicking them and beating them with my fists, talk about hell having no fury. I didn't even think of the consequences, my rage was blind. The girls ran as fast as their legs could carry them. It was fortunate that I was not spotted by the teaching staff. I was sure that I would be to blame, my reputation would have gone before me. From then on, the girls kept their distance from me, but I became a solitary figure, always standing alone in the playground.

My home life was no better. Grace just did not want me there, her taunts were always the same, about my sanity, there was no other way that she could get back at me now. The only time I saw Dad was when he was drunk. He would come into the house, sit himself down in his chair at the side of the fireplace, and immediately fall to sleep. His snores could surely have woken the dead. He was such an uncouth man, he would sit in his chair and spit into the fireplace often missing, making a terrible mess. If he ate cheese sandwiches he would lay newspaper on the table, splash brown sauce everywhere then mop it up with bread. The noise he made whilst eating them was unbelievable, just the sight of him would make me want to shudder.

The nights were no better. I was back in my old room adjacent to theirs. They would make love in a very loud manner, until the early hours of the morning. Since the Staff Nurse at St. Cuthberts had told me about the birds and the bees, I now knew exactly what they were doing, it made me feel sick to the pit of my stomach. They must have known that I could hear them performing. It would have been just as easy for them to have changed rooms with David, who had commandeered the front bedroom across the other side of the landing. The next morning I would feel terribly embarrassed, my face redder than the coals on the fire. I never dared look them in the eyes, I would just rush to get out of the house.

Grace did not want me around too much, and I had not made many new friends for obvious reasons, so I spent a lot of time next door at the drapers talking to Miss Bird, or at my cousin Pat's house.

Pat came to call on me one day, to inform me that our mutual grandmother had died. Grace would not let me attend her funeral, but Pat attends both the funeral and the cremation. The following day she handed me a matchbox. "I've brought you some of Grandma's ashes, because you couldn't attend. I thought you'd like to have them." I gently slid open the box to reveal a heap of grey ashes, and can't conceive that such a fat woman could be condensed to such diminutive proportions. I wept torrents of tears over the matchbox and its contents, and carried it with me everywhere for days. One day, in school, I decided to have a peep, just to make sure that Grandma was still there. "Roberts, what have you got in that matchbox, that is holding your attention so much?" boomed the teacher.

"My Grandma, Miss." The class was in an uproar, the girls were rolling with laughter, tears running down their cheeks.

"Is she Tom Thumb's sister?" one girl spluttered.

"Shut your bloody gobs," I shouted as I rushed from the room, in floods of tears. I'd really set myself up for that one. Would I never learn?

Thursday night was bath night. Gone were the days when we used the tin bath in the middle of the kitchen. We could not supply enough water to fill it, now that the brick copper had gone. So it was down to the slipper baths, where for just a few coppers, one could get a long hot soak, and for a penny extra, perfumed soap was supplied. "Well I'm off then," I told Grace.

"Good, while you're there, see if you can drown yourself, and put us all out of our misery."

"Well at least I wouldn't have to see your ugly face again," I retorted. Whack! The copper stick came crashing down against the back of my head, Grace was out of control. All her pent up feelings of the last few months came to the fore. She could not stop walloping me with the stick. Her face was contorted with hatred. Blood started to pour profusely from a wound in my head, this brought her to her senses. She tried to quell the bleeding, but to no avail. The wound warranted a trip to Casualty.

"This is a really nasty cut, Pearl, I am afraid you will need four or five stitches," the nurse tells me. "Remove your top, and let's clean off some of the blood from your neck." My back is covered in weals from the copper stick, my lip and eyes are now swelling. "How did you get these injuries, Pearl?" the nurse asks, looking concerned.

Quick as a flash Grace replies on my behalf, "She tripped on some worn carpet on the stairs, and fell from top to bottom."

I recall Doctor Mansfield's words, "We will never take you back in St. Cuthberts Pearl."

Weighing up the odds I decided to take a gamble. "She is lying, she has beaten me with the copper stick and I want to see my welfare worker." Grace's look spelt pure hatred, she tried to protest, but the nurse called someone else to watch over me and disappeared, soon returning with a doctor who gave me a brief examination. Turning to Grace he said, "I'm sorry, we must admit the child, we must get in touch with the Welfare."

Later, my wounds attended to, I was placed in a day room with some books to read to await the welfare worker. When she arrived it was obvious that she had been briefed on the situation. A meeting was held with the doctor, Grace, my welfare worker and myself. As usual, Grace shed buckets of tears. "Yes, I did beat her," she admitted. "It was only because I have been at my wits end with her behaviour." Her story continued. "Pearl has been hanging around the gents toilets in the park again, she has also stolen money from my purse. On two occasions I have found pound notes in her pocket, which she can only have stolen from someone. There is no other way that she could have come by amounts of money of that magnitude." My mouth dropped open. None of these accusations were true. Surely Grace could not get away with these lies again? But she did. The hospital discharged me into her care, with the doctor's commiserations. The Welfare said that they would be in touch.

My downfall was that I had not mentioned that anything was amiss with my home life at my fortnightly meetings with the welfare worker, because I still did not trust the authorities. In my mind, it was still possible for them to send me to a mental institution.

Within three days, I found myself in the local Magistrate's Court. I had been brought before them for Grace's allegations, the charge, 'completely out of parental control'. I stood there in the court room, eyes fixed to the floor, shuffling from one foot to the other. I was terrified, surely this meant curtains for me. Grace stood up and spoke her party piece. Her voice filled with great emotion, she said her nerves were suffering as a result of my behaviour. If her nerves were suffering, mine must have been shattered.

The magistrate then asked my opinion. I was so scared I stood and wet myself. In a small muffled, half-sobbing voice I said, "None of it is true, your Royalty." I obviously meant your Honour. "I did not pinch from her purse, or from anyone else's, nor do I hang around outside men's toilets." Then suddenly I cracked, and in a loud panicky voice, I cried, "Please don't send me back to my dad, and please don't send me to a mental home." I felt as though I was fighting for my life, if I didn't speak now, all would be lost.

The members of the bench chatted away for some time with my welfare officer, then the magistrate announced his decision. "We will not be sending you back to your father's home, neither will we be sending you to an asylum, your welfare officer will take care of your placing. Now run along and don't let me see you in front of this court again, child."

Grace's face was a picture. She was obviously expecting something far worse for me. Me, I just felt an overwhelming relief. I did not even say goodbye to Grace, I never wanted to set eyes on her again.

"Why didn't you mention any of this at our fortnightly meetings?" the welfare officer wanted to know as we left the court. I told her that I hadn't been sure, that she wouldn't find me another asylum. "Well Pearl, I have made an emergency placing for you at 'The Beeches', at Kirby Muxloe. It won't be permanent but it will be comfortable for now."

"Then will I go to an asylum?" I asked.

"No Pearl, you will never go back into an asylum."

141

CHAPTER EIGHTEEN

The Beeches is a far cry from my normal dingy existence, the house is palatial, with nicely appointed airy rooms and is set back in large grounds on a main thoroughfare, in one of Leicestershire's wealthiest villages.

The house parents are Mr and Mrs Elveridge, they are kindly people, but strict. They expect a high level of behaviour from the resident children. The first thing that I notice is that the children laugh a lot, this is quite unusual for a children's home. This was the first time that I had been placed in a mixed sex home. There are nine boys and eleven girls. We are extremely well clothed and fed and our bedrooms are comfortable. We are not allowed to call them dormitories, Mrs Elveridge says that the word bedrooms make them sound more homely. We are also allowed to put our own personal stamp on the rooms, such as pictures and ornaments, photographs of family if we have them, unfortunately I have not got any of these things but am very hopeful of acquiring some, because it all seems to me to be such a real privilege.

We have chores to do, but nothing too laborious; the heavy work is carried out by two daily cleaning ladies. Most of our time is spent in our own pursuits, we can wander to the village whenever we like, as long as we behave. Once a week we go to the local cinema, also a local businessman who is a patron of the home, teaches us to horse ride at his private stables. Life is idyllic. I am even allowed to enter the pageant at the Kirby Muxloe Castle ruin. I play a handmaiden and quite take to acting, I really believe it is my forte.

There is a bungalow in the grounds of the house, which was donated by the City Council, it is a replica of a new council house, that has been built in the city. Three children can sleep comfortably inside it, we each have blocks of three nightly sessions. We cook a meal, wash up, make our beds and generally try, with an emphasis on try, to keep the bungalow clean. The idea is to make us independent for later in life, because at sixteen we must leave the protection of the welfare system to fend for ourselves, in outside accommodation, such as board and lodgings or a bedsit. We are not going to have mothers to run around after us like most teenagers.

I'm really happy in this place and manage to behave quite well, I really think my ship has come in. However, as always there is always something to mar my happiness. One morning, Mr Elveridge tells me that he wants a private word with me, I rack my brains thinking what did I do wrong this time. "It's your mother, she is really sick, we are going to take you to visit her," he says.

"Do you mean my real Mum?" I enquire.

"Yes, she is in the Derby Infirmary, we will visit this afternoon."

This was going to be the first time that I had seen my mother since I was four years old, I didn't know what to expect. On arrival, a nurse directed us to a private room where my mother lay. The sight that met me, shocked me to the bone, her head had been shaved, a huge cut was visible at the front of her head, the wound was held together by ugly black stitches and clips. It was just like a scene from a horror movie. Not quite the meeting one would have chosen, after ten years apart. My visit had been arranged because my mother had had a lobotomy operation performed on her brain, the surgeon had suggested that she may not survive. This may be my last chance to visit, although not ideal, and Mr Elveridge did not want it on his conscience.

I was very squeamish, and found it very difficult to look at her, but I knew that I must. Apart from the head wound, I needed to satisfy my curiosity. I had not even seen a photograph of her, any memories which I may have had, had long since faded. I was shocked to find that I did not feel anything for my mother, no love or longing to be with her. All I felt was sorrow that she was sick.

Mr Elveridge explained to me that Dad had given permission for the operation to go ahead, apparently he was still married to her, and therefore, was effectively her next of kin. So Grace was living 'in sin' with my dad, which meant that she wasn't my stepmother. That pleased me tremendously, that evil woman had no part in my life, I could put her out of my mind forever.

Some days after my visit with Mother, I was informed that she had survived and would shortly be going back to the 'mental hospital', as it was now called, the name had certainly gone up market from The City Lunatic Asylum. I could now have regular, supervised visits, but I was in no hurry to take up the offer, new name for the place or not. I was not yet ready to go inside any place like that, my own encounters of the horror of these places were still too fresh in my mind to encounter such visits. Also after seeing her bitterness gradually crept in, subconsciously blaming her for my childhood dilemma.

My remedial time at The Beeches was over, much to my disappointment. I must now move on. I had learnt to laugh again, my high spirits had returned, life was good. The Beeches had been a marvellous experience.

The welfare officer visits to tell me that she has found me a foster home, in an area where no-one will know me. "You will be able to make a fresh start Pearl, and put the past behind you. The people who are taking you in have no idea that you have been in St. Cuthberts.

CHAPTER NINETEEN

This is my big day, I am on my way to my new foster parents, although apprehensive. I am also excited at the prospect of belonging to a real family at last.

We stop outside a small terraced house, in a quiet cul de sac. There is a wonderful aroma of fresh bread in the air, which is coming from the bakery which is situated next door to the house.

As the welfare officer knocks on the door, I nervously step behind her out of view, I feel all at sixes and sevens.

The door is opened to reveal a tall friendly looking lady in her early thirties. "Ha, you've brought Pearl, our foster child." On shaking my hand she introduces herself as Olive. "Come in and meet my mother. She is to be your new guardian, I am her live-in daughter."

We enter a small living room, I am not prepared for the sight that meets me. In the centre of the living room is a double bed, this almost envelops the entire room space. In this bed lies an elderly lady, she is finding it extremely difficult to breathe, each word she speaks comes out with a rasp. The welfare officer notes the look of shock on my face. She attempts to offer me an explanation. "Mrs Law suffers from acute asthma, and cannot climb the stairs, that's why her bed is in the living room." I look embarrassed as Mrs Law struggles to her feet to introduce herself, she is wheezing so badly it is almost too painful to listen to her. As though trying to appease the situation, Olive goes on to explain that she has two sons, Peter and Neil. "They are just a few years younger than you," she explains. "They are at school just now, but will be home shortly."

It is impossible to even begin to understand, how the Welfare Department assessed my placement with these new foster parents. I would have put more thought into baking a fruit cake than the Welfare had done with their investigations. I had just spent a couple of years locked up with old women and now this. I could feel my tummy coming up to meet my throat, the disappointment that I felt was so intense, I could have stood and sobbed.

My feelings had not been considered at all, yet again I was left with a heavy disappointed heart.

The family made me feel welcome, but it was a far cry from what I had envisaged. My imagination had again worked overtime, I'd imagined a wealthy couple in a spacious house, with a lovely garden, who needed a daughter for company. They would take me away on nice holidays to the seaside and join in all sorts of wonderful activities with me, just like I had read in books. Instead, I'd landed in this small terraced house, even smaller than my father's house.

Olive had one bedroom, the boys another and I was accommodated in the box room. The room was clean and pleasant, but a bit on the small side. I chastised myself for being ungrateful, for feeling such disappointment, it may not be The Ritz, but at least they had taken me in. I must make up my mind to make the most of things. At least it was a good deal better than St. Cuthberts.

Olive worked in a local shoe factory, so was away from the house for the whole of the day. I did all I could to help around the house, but Mrs Law was not very talkative to me. There was no spontaneity between us. Although Mrs Law quizzed me often about my former life, I'd immediately clam up; it is not a subject which I am prepared to discuss, if she knew the half of it, she would pack my bags in a thrice. The fact that I would not open up to her, seemed to rile her immensely, often the agitation would bring on another asthma attack, which left me feeling most guilty.

It was with some relief that I got fixed up with a new school, pretty quickly. My new school was 'Crown Hills'. It was a co-educational school, each class had equal numbers of boys and girls, apparently it was a flagship for the city, for a new type of education, as schools in Leicester had always traditionally been one sex only. Much to our pride and joy we were televised on the news, the boys doing cookery and the girls doing woodwork, the school really was progressive.

No one knew my background, neither was there any way that they could find out, so I was immediately accepted by the other pupils and soon began to make friends. I could also throw caution to the wind and not have to be on my guard all of the while, which was a truly great feeling giving me the ultimate in freedom of expression.

The school was rehearsing a play, called Major

Whiskers about a cat that did not wash his whiskers before meals. I auditioned and got the plumb part of Major Whiskers. The play was a resounding success, which brought immediate popularity. At last I was one of the 'in crowd'.

I made a very firm friend, a girl named Marlene Blackwell, and spent many hours at her home, opposite to where I lived. Often I would sleep-over, which was a completely new concept for me. Marlene had many trendy clothes, which she often loaned to me. She styled my hair into the 'D.A', a style where the back of the hair resembled a duck's bum and plastered it down with Brylcreem, to get rid of the horrible frizzy curls that still adorned my head, and which I so much hated. I soon began to look like 'the crowd', and to be accepted by them.

Mo's uncle owned the bakery next door. Mo, (as I now called Marlene), managed to secure me a Saturday job there, I also took an evening paper round, so I had at last got money in my pocket. For the first time ever, I was able to keep up socially with my new found friends. It was a great pity that I also discovered cigarettes at this time. I bought two packets of Park Drive a week, which made a big dent in my wages. But everyone, who was somebody smoked, the advertisements on the cinema explained it all to us, it was the thing to do, we would be cool and sophisticated if we smoked.

It took me three months to get the hang of this smoking lark, each time I lit up I almost turned green and I felt sick, but I had to persevere, otherwise I would be an outsider again. Without exception the whole of the 'in crowd' smoked, when we went out on an evening we popped our cigarettes into long holders adorned with artificial diamanties. Didn't we just think we looked the part. Eventually I got the hang of it, and soon became hooked.

It was not long before I realised that I was very popular with the opposite sex. There was an entry at the side of the house, and I often used it to indulge in many heavy petting sessions. However, I soon learnt that boys were not satisfied with just kissing, they would struggle for far more, but my virginity was one of the things that I was not willing to part with so easily. After all, this was one of the things which Grace had accused me of and which I had vehemently denied. I would never give the authorities the satisfaction of thinking that she had probably been right all along. I was no angel, and often the desire was overwhelming, the closeness of another human being was very exciting and rewarding, after a lifetime of feeling unwanted and untouched, with the exception of violent contact.

Soon I was moving from one relationship to another, as soon as the petting became serious, I would move on to the next lad. I soon found that I was aquiring quite a bad name for myself. I also learnt that if lads didn't score they lied to their friends that they had, just to look macho. This didn't worry me because I became even more popular, often having a waiting list for dates. Wanting to be popular had become like a drug to me, it became worse than any addiction, I just could not abide people disliking me.

Anyway, there was another side to the coin, I dared not get pregnant, otherwise it was possible that I would be locked away forever, this was a risk I was not prepared to take for any lad, even if he had been Prince Charming himself.

Whilst my life outside the house was booming, my life with Mrs Law was not exactly taking off. To be fair, this situation was more my fault than hers. Mrs Law wanted me to stay in the home more to keep her company, but the very thought of the prospect sent me into a fit of depression. We did not have a television like most families round about and there just was nothing to do inside the house, with the exception of reading and I had certainly done enough of that over the proceeding years.

One day, I silently entered the back door and overheard Mrs Law speaking with her friend. "I really wanted a younger girl than Pearl, because after all I've only taken up fostering for the money. Pearl's no company, she's out all the time, God knows where. In two years she'll go, then where will I be? I'll be too old to get another child and the money will dry up, we'll be paupers again."

What a bloody cheek, I thought to myself, and ran over to Mo's house to ask her mum what Mrs Law had meant about the money. "You can't see her today," Mo explained. "She's in bed with the curse." All sorts of weird and wonderful things came to mind, who was cursing her and why?

"What is the curse?" I asked.

"Oh, something to do with her periods," came the

reply. I was still not much the wiser as to why she was cursed because of them, but I had noticed that most of the ladies round about, seemed to take to their bed with this curse. I hope that I don't get this curse, I thought to myself.

The next morning on the way to school, Mo explained to me that Mrs Law gets paid handsomely for fostering me. So that was the angle. I never could figure out why a sick old lady would want the extra burden of a teenage girl. But on reflection she must have earned every penny, having the worry over where I was and what I was doing, and she had offered me a good home, if not ideal for a girl like me.

Six months had passed, I was called to the Welfare Department, which had now taken on a new name, 'The Children's Committee'. I was to go into the city, to Millstone Lane alone. It was an old building set in the back streets, amidst lots of legal offices. "Pearl Roberts, to see the welfare officer," I announced at reception. I was shown into an office where a lady sat behind a desk. She was not my usual welfare worker. "Sit down, I'm Mary Stewart, I am taking over your case. I am new to the area, and am the officer in charge. Would you like a cigarette?" she asks. I'm pretty quick on the uptake and realise that she is testing my honesty. "Yes please," I said.

With an amused twinkle in her eye, she lit a cigarette and passed it over the desk to me. She knows that I know that I'm being tested. I puffed away happily answering all her questions. "You are a bit young at fourteen to smoke Pearl, where do you get your money from?" she asked. I explained about my jobs. "It's a lot of hard work to go up in smoke," she said, but I knew that she would not deter me. The rapport between us was uncanny, particularly as I still had a great dread of anyone in authority, I still felt that they were all out to put me down.

Eventually we got to discuss my present home life. I was apprehensive about telling her how I really felt, but somehow I had a feeling that I could really trust this lady. After listening carefully to what I had to say, she pondered for a short time, tapping her pencil on the desk whilst she thought. "I have the perfect solution for you, it is obvious that you enjoy your school, you are progressing well and your reports are good. You have made many friends in the district, I do not want to disrupt you too much. There is a small children's home around the corner from where you now live. It houses fifteen girls, and is run by a nice lady, who is known as Ma Hammond. I will see if I can get you a placement there."

Within days, Miss Stewart came to visit Mrs Law, and an amicable agreement was reached. I think that Mrs Law was as relieved at the outcome as I was. The move did not bother me in the slightest; I had become accustomed to moving around from one place to another, it had become second nature to me.

CHAPTER TWENTY

Ma Hammond is an elderly spinster, with a heart of gold. All of the girls in her care are happy and carefree. Their ages range between six and sixteen. One girl, Doris, who is fourteen, has been a resident since she was three years old. Ma treats her as though she is her own daughter. Apart from Gerda the German au pair, Ma runs the home single-handed, including doing all the cooking, which is always scrumptious. There is never any food left on plates.

The older girls can go out and about at night, but there is a ten o'clock curfew. Most evenings I hang around the Espresso Coffee bar. I buy two coffees, then I can stay there all evening. All the in crowd meet there. We sit and chat and do the coffee bar jive. The proprietor will not allow us to jig around the floor, as long as we remain seated and continue to buy coffee he allows us to stay. The curfew is moved to eleven o'clock on Saturday nights. This is always our big night out. First it's round to Mo's house where we spend ages getting ready. Then we plaster our faces with make up and then dress ourselves in our dirndle skirts, which we make stick out with heavily starched net under slips. On go the stiletto heels, which we can hardly walk in, and we totter off to the dance hall.

We bop the night away, always keeping our eyes peeled for any new male talent, we are usually successful. Mo is very dark, and I am very blonde, so we complement each others' looks. There is no alcohol sold at the dance hall, only soft drinks, but this does not worry us unduly. We are really only here for the lads. We leave about ten o'clock, have a quick snog with one of the lads we have met, on the way home, then run like hell to get me home by eleven o'clock. I usually make it by the skin of my teeth. Ma is usually waiting on the doorstep to make sure I have not trailed home any 'unsavoury characters'. This is what she calls the 'Teddy Boys', who dress in their drape suits.

My school days are nearly over. I have just sat the School Certificate, and am awaiting my results. Most of my friends are not too bothered because they have decided to take jobs in factories, that's where the money is. A factory job does not appeal to me at all. Listening to the radio one day, I hear the word telegraphist. I like the word, look it up in the dictionary, then decide that's what I want to be. I consult Miss Stewart , she says I must wait for my results. Some days later they arrive, I have done extremely well, my qualifications are high enough to become a telegraphist. Miss Stewart is highly pleased with my results, she said my marks were astounding, given my past circumstances, also they were unusual for a girl in care. "I will back you all the way, you must have worked really hard."

Unfortunately there were no vacancies for telegraphists, so I opted for the next best thing, a Post Office Telephonist. Miss Stewart arranged and accompanied me to my interview, which I passed with flying colours, except for vocabulary, my speech consisted of pure Leicester dialect. If I was willing to take elocution lessons for three months, then the job was mine.

Ma had allowed me to celebrate my fifteenth birthday with a party, six guests are allowed to be invited, there is no room for any more. I'm so excited, this will be the first party ever held in my honour. My friends arrive, laden with presents and records to play on the record player, Johnny Ray, Tommy Steele and Elvis blare out until eleven thirty. It had been a perfect evening, I retired to bed exhausted but happy.

My papers arrived from the Post Offiice. I was to start at the training school in September. I could hardly wait to get started, my elocution lessons were coming along well. I walked around all day sounding my vowels and repeating, "Mum makes Madeira most mornings." I really fancied myself with my new posh sounding accent.

I wasn't a bit nervous on my first day at work. I felt so proud. Me, Pearl Roberts, the 'nutter' landing a job like this. Who would have thought it fifteen months ago. I eagerly grasped each challenge as it came, and was soon ready for my first day in the switch room. Dressed in a smart blouse, with grey pencil skirt and white ankle socks, I took my place at the switchboard. My keenness was so acute, I even wore my headset whilst eating my lunch in the canteen, much to everyone's amusement.

Once a week I went to college on day-release, employees under sixteen were only allowed to work so many hours per week, therefore the day at college compensated. I studied accounts, bookbinding and sword fencing. I continued to make progress, sat my civil service examination and received quite good results, life was going very well.

My earnings were three pounds, nineteen shillings and sixpence per week, a princely sum in the fifties. I gave Ma three pounds towards my keep, she gave me back my bus fare to work each day, to make sure that I did not spend it on trivialities. Most days I would walk the three miles to work, this gave me extra money for my cigarettes. I could now afford to but a packet of five cigarettes a day.

One Saturday night at the Trocodero, I met a boy who I fancied, he told me that he attended the church youth club every Thursday night. As I lived next door to the church I thought I would call in, perhaps he would ask me for a date. He did and I became a firm member of St. Stephens Church. It was great fun. Once a month we would have a youth breakfast after morning service, we would all take our own eggs and bacon and cook the meal. After breakfast was over, we would have a choir practice, the youth of the church sang at charity events. Ma was more than happy that I had got in with the 'right crowd', as she put it. "Better than hanging around that coffee bar," she sniffed.

It was almost Christmas; we in the choir had learnt all our Christmas carols. The aim was to go around the streets with collecting boxes, singing. The money was to go to the upkeep of the church. With our lanterns and hymn books we set off, it was great fun in the dark. Most of the houses we called at offered us a mince pie and a glass of sherry. I had never touched alcohol before, and after just a few drinks I was merry. The other choir members thought that this was hilarious, they kept feeding me more, and by the end of the night I was paralytic. My dear church friends left me propped up against a wall, and went home. No way would the 'in crowd' have done this to me, they would have supported me and sobered me up. Eventually the police picked me up. I managed to give them my name and address, then passed out. It was almost midday before I was fully awake, never had I seen Ma so angry. "The shame of it, the police at my door, bringing one of my girls home in such a state. You will not have heard the last of this," she continued. It was pointless telling my side of the story, it seemed too improbable. Ma was right, two days later the police again arrived at the door. "Because of the state you were in on Friday night, we are going to prosecute you for under age drinking."

The following week I was brought before the Juvenile Court. In summing up, the magistrate said that in view of my past, he could not ignore this incident. "You will serve six months in a remand centre. Mary Stewart tried very hard to fight my corner, but to no avail. My voice rang out in the silent courtroom, "No, please don't do this to me, I'll be good, please give me one more chance. I won't do it again, please," I begged.

The magistrate just looked at me with distaste and said, "Take her away."

I was appointed a probation officer named Miss

Belbarda, who was to take me to Breadsall in Derbyshire. I was heartbroken, the whole of the last eighteen months had been in vain. Once again, I got this isolated feeling, and with a shudder, I wondered if this was going to be the pattern of my life forever. To find happiness and then have it snatched away from me, even though most of the mistakes were caused not only by circumstances but by my own out and out stupidity.

CHAPTER TWENTY ONE

Breadsall Remand Home was set in the rolling hills of the Derbyshire countryside, the views were absolutely breathtaking, if I had been taking a holiday there, I would have been more than satisfied. However, any romantic notions that I had of the place soon disappeared when I entered the house.

I didn't like the Matron the second I set eyes on her. She was a manly sort of woman, who wore manly types of clothes, there was nothing feminine about her at all. Her hair was cut so short, that it must certainly have been styled by an army barber. She didn't walk, she strutted, taking heavy deliberate strides. Her first words were, "Roberts, this is not a holiday centre, you are here to repent your sins, and your sins you will repent." I then received the normal welcome institutional lecture, all the dos and don'ts. The list of rules was so long that it would have taken Einstein to remember them all. "No need to bath you, you will be clean coming straight from a children's home, not like some of the filthy brats I get in here," she said. "They wouldn't know what a bath was if you threw them in one."

"Charming," I thought to myself.

I was issued with a uniform, it was so dowdy, that the thought of wearing it made me even more depressed. I was craving for a cigarette, but had had them confiscated along with all my other personal items.

"You own nothing here Roberts, everything is mine, get used to it," Matron informed me.

My bedroom was small, I was to share with three other girls, Mary, Ena and Susan. They tried to make conversation on the first night, but I was in no mood to socialise. I laid on my back staring at the ceiling, I knew that we all had our cross to bear, but this felt more like the crucifixion, the pain I felt was so hard to bear. Why did everything always go wrong for me? I laid there and wallowed in self pity, eventually crying myself to sleep.

I didn't have much time to wallow the next morning though, a bell sounded at six o'clock, my room mates were out of bed like bullets being fired from a rifle. "Don't lay there," they warned. "Warden will be round in a minute, if you're still in bed you'll be for it."

The house was freezing cold as we made our way to the showers, dressed only in our cotton night gowns. A queue had already formed, apparently there was always a race to get to the showers every morning, the reason being that the first out and dressed got the best chores. Three of the girls were pregnant, but they were still forced to strip off in front of the rest of us, all of their dignity was being taken away, usually the only reason that they were there was because they had got themselves pregnant in the first place. "Paying for the lust of the body Roberts," Matron said pointing at their undressed bodies. "Let these girls be a lesson to you." I'm sure she took great delight in ogling them, her eyes would narrow and her mouth go into a sneer. "Roberts, you are on toilet and laundry duty today, you've got one and a half hours, so get cracking." I thought that this was going to be easy considering that I had been almost last in line. It was a shock to learn that laundry didn't mean putting the clothes into a machine and watching them rotate, then removing them to hang them on the line, it meant scrubbing the cobbled laundry floor in the basement. We were to scrub and polish each cobble until you could see your face in them, a pointless task really, no one else but us saw these silly cobbles.

My work mate, Chris, was only thirteen and was one of the girls who was heavily pregnant, she told me that she had been a prostitute in Birmingham for a year. It may seem naive of me, but she needed to explain to me what a prostitute actually did, because I hadn't the vaguest idea.

The sound of a gong indicated that breakfast was being served. "Quick, empty the buckets, if we are more than three minutes late, we are not allowed to eat," indicated Chris. We had three flights of stairs to climb before reaching the canteen, by the time we got there Chris was puffing like and old steam train, but we made it. The dash was worthwhile because the breakfast was more than substantial.

The rest of the morning was taken up with schooling. I was not keen on this, I had thought that I had put my school days behind me. Most of the lessons were boring, I'd covered all the topics before, but some of the girls could not even read and write, so I supposed the lessons were good for them, even help them later on the outside.

There was a nice view from the window where I was sitting, and I spent more time concentrating on the wild life in the garden than listening to the teacher. Squirrels ran around playing antics jumping from tree to tree, sitting with their little paws full of food munching away, it was a delight to watch them and certainly whiled away the hours.

After lunch it was gardening time, weeding and picking up garden debris. Mary, my room mate, beckoned me to follow her. "Just showing Roberts where the toilet is," she shouted over to the watching warden. We walked to the back of the trees. Once in the toilet, Mary stood on the toilet seat and pulled a packet of Park Drive and a box of Swan Vestas from the back of the cistern. "I get me Mam to smuggle them in for me every visiting day," she told me. "You can share them with me, if you share everything that you get from your visitors." I told her that it was highly unlikely that I would get any visitors, but feeling sorry for me she still agreed to share.

"Only smoke half at a time, that way they'll last the week. We have to come into the garden rain or shine. Eat a leaf of mint afterwards, then no one will smell the tobacco on your breath." At least that was my cigarette problem solved to some extent.

Each night after lights out, we played a game, whereby every girl told a true story about their lives. There were certain aspects of mine which I obviously was not about to reveal. It came to the night, when the story to be told was about sex, my room mates came up with the most amazing stories of their sexual

163

encounters, my eyes almost bulged out of my head, I had no idea that such things happened. Although I was the eldest in the room, as mentioned before, I had never been sexually active, this made me feel inadequate. I took a mixture of their stories, added a little spice then flowered them up and told my story. "Roberts!" a voice boomed. "Whatever do you think you are playing at teaching filth to girls younger than yourself?" Matron had crept upon us, wearing her bedroom slippers. Apparently she often listened in on bedtime conversations, but no one had thought to warn me. That night we had not heard her approach. I was yanked from my bed and frog-marched down the stairs to the showers. Matron stripped me off and turned the cold shower on full. "There, that will cool your ardour, don't let me ever hear filth spill from your mouth again. Now put your night dress back on and come to my office."

Talk about bad luck, four stories had been told, and mine was the only one which had been overheard, possibly the only one that had been untrue. Back in her office I was lectured on the corrupt mind. Matron told me that she had read all the data in my files. "I did not believe what I had read about your sexual perversions in your early life. Now I can see they were true, I think you are depraved Roberts." Trying to explain was useless, every time I opened my mouth to say anything she shouted me down. My story was once again left untold. It never seemed to occur to her that it was unlikely that I could teach these younger girls anything, given the pregnancy of one of them and their illicit trade of their bodies did not seem to deter her, she was just hell bent on blaming me.

That night I was put into another bedroom with girls more my own age, they had carried out such crimes that warranted a prison sentence, but they were too young to serve in an adult prison. What I didn't know about crime I soon learned, after a couple of months I knew every trick in the book.

My behavioural pattern began to alter so much that Matron sent for my probation officer, Miss Belbarda. On arrival she was appalled at my change in attitude. "Pearl whatever has happened to you, please don't harden yourself to the world, you only have three months left to do in here." She then went on to explain that she was trying to convince Ma Hammond that I deserved a second chance. "But with your changed attitude, you don't stand a cat in hell's chance, just buck your ideas up and show us some of that pluck for which you are renowned and as up to now pulled you through the bad times."

The visit brought rewards, for that night I had a change of bedroom, which pleased me, I have to confess that I was a little afraid of the former girls. My new room mates were only serving time for petty incidents such as my own. After Miss Belbarda's visit, and with something to look forward to, I learnt to keep my head down and co-operated as much as possible, which I often found very difficult because Matron was such a vicious woman. It had been known for girls to wet their knickers just at the sound of her voice, which was not surprising as her voice could only be likened to a fog horn, sounded in the English Channel on a misty day. The girls nicknamed her 'Mein Helga'. I suppose on reflection that she had to be a hard woman given the nature of some of the girls in her care, a softer woman would have been literally eaten alive.

Once a week, the wardens would take us down into the village to post any letters which we may have written. The postmistress watched us like a hawk to make sure we didn't pinch any of her displayed goodies. The walk was refreshing and we always wanted to go whatever the weather.

The remand home was really for a short sharp shock, to put us on the right road to being decent citizens, so it had to be tough or the detention would have been pointless. So the short sharp shock treatment was actually invented in the early fifties.

Soon my time at Breadsall was up and Miss Belbarda was coming to drive me back to Leicester. It was a great relief to be leaving the place, I had had no inclination to make any firm friends there, so I would never look back on those six months with any affection. As Miss Belbarda put it, "Just look at the episode as a small blip in your life, Pearl."

CHAPTER TWENTY TWO

The drive back to Leicester was a pleasant one, we stopped off at Matlock, to partake of a cream tea and have a wander round. Miss Belbarda told me that I was being returned to Ma Hammond, however I could not have my job back at the Post Office, the Civil Service did not employ people who have committed any sort of crime. "It is unfortunate, but there you are," she said. "You must keep your nose clean this time Pearl, or you will end up in a far worse institution than you have just left. There will be no further chances for you, stop being so vulnerable and start being your own person, just do not listen to other people so much."

Ma did not show any recrimination against me, she just accepted me back into her fold without any lectures, she possibly thought that I had been given them all, and that my six months in the remand home had been enough to calm me. It felt great to be 'home'. Soon I was back in with the crowd and was even more popular than I had been before, I had so many stories to relate about the remand home, what wasn't fact I made up. I dined on lots of free coffee over the coming months, as my friends sat agog listening. With the help of my probation officer I soon secured another job as a telephonist at a local shoe factory. It was here that I met my lifelong friend Sheila Fritche. Sheila was one of the very few people to whom I have told my life story. She did not hold it against me, but just accepted me for what I was, lively and full of fun.

We became friends both inside and outside of work, she took me to meet her parents who were very kind to me. Because of the night curfew at Ma's, Sheila's mum Kath, let me stay at their house at the weekends. This enabled us to go into town to the *Palais De Dance* for the Saturday night bash. Rock and Roll was now all the rage. Sheila could dance it tremendously well and soon taught me lots of the steps, but I could not hold a candle to her dancing.

She was very popular because of her skill, and all the lads wanted to dance with her, so again, I soon became one of the in crowd. On Sundays we went to the Market Square where the speakers took their forum. We didn't go to listen but to heckle, we found this highly amusing, but it was all innocent fun. We really fancied ourselves as townies. My one great wish was to own a pair of drainpipe trousers and a drape coat.

At lunchtime Sheila and I went to a cafe near the factory, this was owned by two men, Paul and Jim. We got very friendly with Jim's wife Margaret and the five of us had a good laugh every lunchtime. We always asked for a good square meal and a round of toast. We would then toss a coin to see whether we would pay that day or at the end of the week. Sheila and I usually won, and very rarely settled our bill. Paul told me that I should have a date with him to compensate, but I turned him down because of the nine years age difference.

I decided to continue my education by taking evening classes at the local college. Whilst browsing through the notice board one evening, a card caught my eye. 'Wanted female nude models for still-life class, two pounds per hour.' That's it, I can do that, I thought, I would soon have enough money for my drainpipe trousers. The thought of stripping off didn't unduly bother me, after all, so many doctors had looked at my body it was almost a museum piece, I reasoned. I went to the bursar's office for the interview. The art teacher gave me the once over, being so slim, he said I was ideal for the job. "Start tomorrow at seven," he said.

Seven o'clock on the dot I was sitting naked on the desk, it was all done in a very discreet manner. Once the lesson was over, I nipped along to the refectory for some refreshment. To my astonishment I bumped into my cousin Eric. He was studying to become a surveyor. "What are you doing here? he enquired, my face must have looked just like a beetroot, I was sure that he knew what I'd been up to just by looking at me. It was the last thing I wanted to get out, if it had got back to the Children's Committee I would have been done for. "Just taking a bookkeeping course," I sheepishly replied. "Do you take art classes as part of your course? I asked him, fortunately he didn't.

I continued with my modelling, making sure I remained discreet. Very soon I had saved up sufficient money to buy my clothes. Once I had them I gave in my notice at the college. If Ma had found out she would have frowned upon it, I could almost hear her saying, "Exposing your body to the world, it just isn't lady like."

Drainpipe trousers had to be worn very tight, so before wearing them I needed to undo all the stitching from the knee down, then stitch them up whilst wearing them, this was a tedious task, but I felt sure that it was worthwhile. Although I was ultra slim, I had a good pair of legs and the drainpipes showed them off a treat. Rightly or wrongly I thought I was the best thing since sliced bread, and that I was sex appeal on legs.

The first time that I wore them I felt tougher, taller and self confident. The old adage 'clothes maketh man', was certainly true in my case. Sheila and I would go into town, and if anyone looked at us, we would rudely sneer, "Do you want a picture?" We would stand on the street corner singing Teddy Boy tunes, passers-by would cross to the other side of the street. Sheila's mum would have been appalled. To us it was just a bit of fun and we meant no harm. If there had been any trouble we would have been off like a shot. Because of my new attire, I began to associate with the 'Teddy Boy Gang', and soon fell hopelessly in love with a tall blond haired chap called Doug. This was my first experience in an in-depth relationship, I couldn't eat or sleep and just counted the hours between each date, where I would sit and listen to him all dewy eyed, hanging onto his every word, all but drooling at the mouth.

We would go to the cinema and miss most of the film because we were too busy petting on the back row. He would shake with emotion. He told me that he loved me and of course I believed him, especially with there being such a shortage of love before, in my young life. "Let's go," he muttered one night in the middle of the film. He led me along the railway track to a small hut, where we began to pet heavily. He soon became very excited and tried to make me submit to him, but I could just not make that final commitment. I pulled myself up from the ground and ran away sobbing, tripping over and tearing my drainpipes as I ran. He was in hot pursuit, all sorts of imaginings passed through my head, and I ran even harder. At last he caught up, "Don't worry Pearl, it's okay," was all he said, then offered to escort me home.

That night I could not sleep and walked the room restlessly, should I have submitted? I wasn't sure. I was no angel, I really hankered after that human touch, the passion within me burned, like nothing I had ever experienced before, I could not understand the demands that my body was asking of me, the feelings were so alien, but for once my head had ruled my heart, now I was sure that I would lose Doug. I laid on the bed musing, when I heard voices speaking in whispers below my window, I recognised one as Gerda's. Creeping to the window, I peered through the curtains, the sight I saw was most unwelcome, there stood Gerda petting heavily with Doug. I flew down the stairs two at a time into the back garden and confronted them, they told me that they had been an item for some weeks. "What about me, what about our dates? I screamed at Doug. He turned to Gerda and told her that he didn't know what I was talking about. "Liar, liar?" I shouted, thumping Doug on his chest. He just held me at arm's length and pushed me away. Total disdain on his face. "You're just a kid," he retorted. "I don't mess with kids." The total rejection of this, my first love mortified me, I could not stop in that place and see them together, having their intimacy rubbed into my face. My heart felt as though it was breaking, for once, I thought I had found someone who really did love me, and not just make believe for their own ends.

That night became a completely sleepless one, I just tossed and turned and by morning I had hatched my plan.

"Ma, can I have my bank book please? I am to get a bonus at work, but the boss wants to put it straight into my bank account."

Without question Ma took it from her safe saying, "Don't lose it, it's your future." It is common practice for working girls in care to have savings deducted from their board to see them on their way, when they leave the home.

"Sheila! I want to talk to you in the cloakroom, it's urgent." Curiosity got the better of her and she came rushing over. "What's the matter?" she asked.

"I'm running away to London, I'm going to the Post Office to draw out my savings." I explained to her about Doug and Gerda, she did all in her power to dissuade me from going, but my mind was made up. I asked her to cover for me while I slipped out of work.

With my money in my pocket, I made my way to

the train station and did not have to wait long for the London train. Tears wet my cheeks as the train pulled out of the station. "Goodbye Leicester," I murmured, I was acting like a drama queen at her first performance. I was half expecting Doug to run alongside the train declaring his undying love. Of course that was impossible for he didn't even know that I was running away.

My conviction to run away was not quite as strong when I reached London. I travelled around on the underground for most of the day, not quite knowing what my next move should be. Night was fast approaching, the thoughts of sleeping on the streets terrified me. Eventually I reached a place in the suburbs and decided to book into a small hotel. I chose one called *'The Tudor'*, explaining to the proprietor that I was on a course at the London Telephone Exchange. She showed me to a single room, where I slept soundly until the early hours of the morning. At first light, I climbed out of the window and nipped off without paying. I needed to conserve the little cash that I had.

The days that followed were adventurous, seeing all the sights of London. Each night I chose a different hotel to sleep in, each time I was lucky to get a downstairs room. After six nights my luck ran out. The proprietor of the hotel in which I was stopping got suspicious about a young girl being alone in London on a course. He called the police. When they turned up I tried to make a run for it, but was not quick enough. After some questioning it became evident to them that I was a runaway.

"Down to the station with you young madam." Stubbornness prevented me from giving the policeman my name. "You'll be put into the cells until you do tell us," the constable told me harshly, just the mention of the word cell changed my mind. "Pearl Roberts, from Leicester," I offered. He located me on the missing persons list. Apparently, back in Leicester Sheila had been interviewed by the police and had felt obligated to tell them where I had gone for my own safety.

The police fed me, made a few telephone calls, then escorted me to the train station. "Don't get any clever ideas about getting off the train, there will be a constable on every station along the route."

He was right. At each station the train stopped at, there was a policeman standing on the platform. The train eventually chugged into the Leicester station, where there was a reception committee to meet me. The police were there, my probation officer, Ma from the home and Mary Stewart. By this time everyone had gleaned most of the story as to why I'd run away.

Miss Stewart explained to me that she was sending me away to another city, to make yet another fresh start. She understood my heartbreak but felt that while I remained in Leicester, I would only hanker after Doug. Once again I pleaded with Miss Stewart to allow me to stay, but she said it wasn't possible. Ma Hammond had given up on me and no longer wanted me to stay in her home.

Who would have thought that something as innocent as a pair of drainpipe trousers were to be yet another downfall for me.

CHAPTER TWENTY THREE

Today I was introduced to my new probation officer, Miss Gough. Her first task was to escort me to Leeds on the train. Mary Stewart had found me a place in a Salvation Army hostel for working girls.

The hostel was set in an old part of Leeds, where the houses were back to back. Never before had I seen washing hanging across the street. The hostel itself was an old rambling building, clean but very basic. My first impression was not a good one. There was not a homely atmosphere like at Ma's, I wanted to turn and run. The place was not my scene at all.

Major ran the home along with three other Salvationists, they were all friendly but cool. The residents were all away at work, and would not return until after six o'clock. Major told me that my first priority was to find a job, all the girls at the hostel had to work, even if it meant lowering my sights. "Beggars cannot be choosers," she quoted. "You have blotted your copy book, you must now pay the price."

The girls began to trickle in from work and the place began to buzz. Once they were all home, the hostel took on a different atmosphere. The girls appeared to be older and maturer than myself, though I was not renowned for my maturity in any event. A tall, buxom girl approached me. "Hi, I'm Sally, you are sharing with me and two others, stick by me kid and you'll be alright."

The following day I went to the labour exchange, this was the first time that I had had to look for work on my own. There was still plenty of work to be had in the fifties, and I secured an interview for that afternoon. I arrived at 'Lillies of Leeds', a high class furnishing ironmongers, half an hour before my appointed interview time. I sat outside the manager's office shaking in my boots. I was scared to death. Exactly on the stroke of two, the manager's door opened. "Ha, I see you are a good timekeeper, Roberts."

The interview went well and I secured the position of sales girl and Appliance Demonstrator. "No need to dally over your starting date, be here tomorrow at eight thirty." And at eight thirty the next morning, I was there. It was a nice store, it smelled of paraffin and polish, and I was put in the electrical appliance department. Most of the staff were dreadfully posh, and I must have stuck out like a sore thumb. It did enter my head to wonder why the manager had given me the position. My departmental head, Miss Sylvia Salisbury, told me that I had been successful because I looked clean and didn't wear oodles of make up.

I soon settled down and got on well with the rest of the staff, although they were all much older than myself. There were only two youngsters in the shop, a young lad called Malcolm and I. We were both teased unmercifully, constantly being asked to fetch pints of virgin water and the like. It was all good clean fun and it didn't bother me in the least.

Some Saturdays we attended shows where we

would exhibit the goods. My favourite was the Harrogate Show, it was the first time that I was to demonstrate. The product was the Philishave Rotary Shaver. I was to stand at the end of the stall and sing a small ditty. "Shave with perfection, with the rotary action, shave with Philishave today." Then I demonstrated the shaver on men's faces. It was such good fun. The manager was so pleased with me, he gave me a bonus in my pay packet that week.

On Saturday nights, a few girls from the hostel would go out dancing in Leeds. Sally would do herself up in the tightest of clothes, when she walked her bottom would wriggle so much it could have caused a traffic jam. She simply oozed sex appeal. Every week she picked up a different guy and then vanished for a couple of hours. In bed later, she'd tell me about her date. Deep down she was a very lonely person, like me, she never discussed her past. Sally and I had nothing to do with the other two girls who shared our room. They were lesbians and often embarrassed us with their antics. Little was known about this subject in the fifties and this was my first experience of it.

On two occasions Major found them in bed together, and on each occasion all hell let loose. Sally and I were dragged into the Major's office, where we got a dressing down for not reporting the two girls. However, this would not have been possible, we might have received a knife in our backs, they were two tough cookies. It was a case of put up and shut up. We just put our heads under the sheets and pretended that it wasn't happening. At least they were so involved with each other, that Sally and I were safe. Often, I would wonder whether Miss Stewart was aware of the sort of girls that resided at this home. Sally and I did ask for a move to another room, but we were told there was no space elsewhere.

"Letter for you, Pearl," Major called one evening when I returned home from work.

"Thanks, the handwriting is not familiar," I replied. On opening the letter I found that it was from Paul, the chap who owned the cafe in Leicester where Sheila and I used to have a good 'square meal'.

"Dear Pearl," the letter began. "I have dearly missed you coming into the cafe at lunchtime and would like to come and visit you, there in Leeds." The rest of the letter just contained trivia.

"Sally, what do you think of this letter?" I asked her at suppertime, handing it to her to read.

"Go for it Pearl, invite him up for a visit, he seems keen."

I replied to Paul's letter straight away. In Paul's next letter he arranged to visit me in two weeks time. "Hey Sally, what's an attache? Paul says he is going to bring one with him."

"Bet it's some kind of dog," she replied. Sally and I trailed around Leeds looking for a guest house that would accommodate a man and his dog, we eventually found a guest house and booked it.

On the way to work a few days later, I noticed that there was to be a sale at the Co-operative store. There in front of the window was a beautiful two piece pink suit in a size ten, just my size, for just one pound. I knew I'd got to have it for my date. On the day of the sale I cleared it with Major and set off to the store at four o'clock in the morning, walking all the way into Leeds. There were already other people queuing, but after enquiring, it appeared that no one else wanted the suit. The doors opened at nine a.m. on the dot. I ran inside there like Roger Bannister running the four minute mile. With relief, I secured the suit. Later that day, I paraded in front of Sally. "What do you think?" I asked.

"You look great kid, you'll knock him dead," she replied.

The weekend of the date arrived. There I was at the train station waiting for Paul's train to arrive, dressed up in my nice pink suit. Paul alighted from the train, but no dog. After the usual greetings, I asked, "Where is your little dog?"

"What little dog?" he said.

"You said you were bringing your attache." He looked mesmerised, no wonder, I found out later than an attache was a case, just wait until I got my hands on Sally!

We had a wonderful weekend, Paul was the perfect gentleman. He told me lots about himself, I learned that he was a colonial born in India, and he had come to Britain after the fall of Raj. It all sounded very romantic and exciting. All too soon, the weekend was over and Paul was on his way back to Leicester. Nothing had been said about any future dates.

Some days later, a letter arrived, this time I recognised the handwriting. "Dear Pearl, I enjoyed my weekend so much, I would like to marry you, etc. etc." I was absolutely gob-smacked, I rushed off to find Sally. "What do you think to this?" I asked, showing her my letter.

"Crikey, go for it kid, you don't get many offers like that to the pound."

The next day I wrote my acceptance. I also wrote to Mary Stewart in Leicester telling her of my intentions, she must have caught the very next train. On her arrival, we sat and had a long talk. Paul had to meet with her approval before the engagement could go ahead. He had to attend meetings at the Children's Department and go in front of a panel to be vetted for his suitability. He must find suitable accommodation and meet all of their requirements. As I was only sixteen, I was still classed as a juvenile. Within weeks, the answer came through, Miss Stewart and her colleagues had found him suitable.

I went to see the priest in Leeds and arranged my pre-nuptial lessons, which I was to attend every Thursday. On returning home from work one Thursday evening, Major called me into her office, "A man called on the telephone to speak to you today, he can't make it tonight. You're nothing but a hussy, getting engaged to one man, and dating another. I shall have to write and tell your intended," she admonished.

"Don't do that," I pleaded. "The man was a priest." But she didn't believe me. Frantically I called the priest and asked him to ring the Major to explain. This he must have done whilst I was at work the following day.

We were all sat down for our evening meal when Major came to join us, which was most unusual. Rapping the table, she called for silence. "Pearl Roberts, stand on the table." Stunned, I obeyed. She went on, "This girl is a Catholic, she is not fit to eat Salvation Army bread and butter, she can no longer stay here."

I was amazed, I had always thought that Salvationists were tolerant of any faith. I couldn't believe that I was being thrown out of a home because of my religious background.

The following day, Mary Stewart came to fetch me. She told me that she had found me a place in a convent. Laughingly she chided, "At least this is the last time that I will have to find you a placement, which is good, because I am running out of ideas."

181

CHAPTER TWENTY FOUR

There was a warm feeling of serenity encircling St. Teresa's Convent, a feeling that one needed to be at peace with the world, a far cry from the hustle and bustle of the Salvation Hostel.

Mother Superior extended her hand in welcome, turning to Mary Stewart she said, "Pearl will find peace in this place, in preparation for her forthcoming marriage, time to reflect on her past life, and cleanse herself for the future." The poetic words embarrassed me slightly and I found myself blushing deeply.

There was a little bell on the hall table which Mother Superior rang, within seconds a very young nun appeared, her beauty was stunning. "Sister Maria will show you to your room, I am sure you will find it most comfortable." Taking up my holdall, containing all my worldly goods, we followed Sister Maria up three flights of stairs. "This is your room, I do hope you like it." The room was well appointed, not plush but comfortable, and immediately I stepped inside the room, I knew that I could never live in it. There was no window just a small skylight. We stood chatting, I was finding it difficult to breathe, my head was beginning to spin, this room reminded me of the padded cell at St. Cuthberts.

Miss Stewart noticed the look of sheer panic on my face. "Leave me alone with Pearl for a few moments please, I think she feels unwell." Once alone she asked me what the problem was. I knew I had to tell her, there was no other option. A look of sympathy crossed her face. "Come with me, I will talk with Mother Superior." I all but ran down the stairs. "Is it possible for Pearl to walk in the garden for a while, she feels a little faint?" Miss Stewart suggested. The garden was beautiful, there was a small but eye catching grotto in a quiet corner in which stood a statue of 'The Virgin Mary'. Two sisters sat beside her on a bench reading, the scene was one of pure tranquillity, almost like a scene from 'The Nun's Story'. They bade me to sit beside them.

After a while, I began to feel calmer, but concerned. Where would I go if there was no alternative room? Mother Superior appeared at the French window, "We have found you another room with a larger window, Pearl." This room was perfect.

Immediately outside my bedroom door was the convent altar, where the nuns held various Masses, for some obscure reason I felt the need to creep by. Meals were eaten in the convent refectory, cooked and served by the nuns. Each meal had to be ordered in advance and could only be eaten at set times. Because there were no common rooms, the refectory was the only place where it was possible to meet some of the other paying guests, who were mostly middle aged working ladies. Transistor radios could not be played in the bedrooms, it was almost possible to hear the silence. I imagined that life could be very lonely here, and hoped that my stay would not be for too long.

When Miss Stewart left, Sister Maria gave me a

front door key, and informed me that the door would be bolted at eleven thirty each evening, unless by prior arrangement. It seemed that I was now to take charge of my own life, which made me feel a little afraid.

Once alone in my room, the serenity did not feel so inviting. I had not been left alone to take care of my own affairs for quite some time. Pulling on my coat, I decided to visit Paul, he had no idea on what day I was to arrive as the move back to Leicester had all happened so quickly. The delighted look on his face at my sudden appearance was most rewarding. The noise of the busy little cafe was far more to my liking, with the coming and going of the customers.

My first duty was to find work to enable me to pay for my keep. I was spoilt for choice with numerous jobs at the Labour Exchange, but eventually decided on a showroom job at a local electrical wholesalers. I really welcomed the work to keep me occupied. The pay was not too bad and I could earn bonuses, unfortunately breakages for broken glass shades had to be paid for, and I broke so many, that I never did get a bonus, I think that I must have owed the company more money than I earned.

Paul worked until eleven o'clock most evenings in his cafe, to accommodate the teenagers coming back from the town. He wouldn't let me help because most of the customers were usually the worse for drink. I think that the real reason though was because I knew most of the lads from my past.

Being seventeen years old, I got pretty bored waiting around for Paul, so I spent most of my time with my old girl friends. With the exception of Sister Maria, I had no-one to talk to at the convent. Maria often came to my room and we would sit on my bed and discuss topical things, I must admit though, these conversations bore little resemblance to my normal conversations, which were normally about the latest pop group and films. On the odd nights that I did stay in, I felt very lonely.

Goods news arrived. The Children's Committee had decided that I could get married in December, that was only three months to go. There were lots of preparations to make. The Committee were to pay for my wedding attire and trousseau, and Paul was going to pay for the reception.

Miss Gough and the Children's Committee took me into town to all the best shops and bought me four sets of clothes. "To set you up for your new life Pearl, we can't have you leaving us with no clothes to your back," Miss Gough said. Next was the wedding gown shop, where we purchased a beautiful white gown covered in pretty lace and pearls, a long veil and a tiara. I could not believe how fortunate I was.

The Church had been booked and the five bridesmaids had been chosen, the Committee was certainly pushing the boat out to make my day extra special. There were only the invitations to send out. This posed somewhat of a problem from my point of view, Paul knew exactly which guest he wished to attend from his side. It crossed my mind that I really ought to invite my dad. No matter what, we only have one father, I argued to myself, but the invitation could not possibly include Grace, the thought of her attending my wedding abhorred me.

The only way to contact my dad on his own, was to track him down at one of his drinking venues. I took the decision to go and search for him alone. Eventually I found him drinking in the Midland Hotel, a local pub near his home. I asked around for John Roberts as I did not think I would be able to identify him. He was pointed out to me and I was alarmed to see that he was surrounded by women. It took courage, but I cautiously approached him. "Hello." I was about to say 'Dad', when he pulled me onto his knee and inquired as to what night he'd had me. I was appalled, he hadn't even recognised me, and had mistaken me for one of his floozies. Struggling to free myself from him, I made myself known to him before leaving. The look on his face was one of astonishment, he was crossed off my wedding list without hesitation or any further feelings of guilt.

Just a few weeks later, Paul and I were walking through the city centre shortly after closing time, when my dad walked out of a public house renowned for its dubious clientele, with a buxom woman on each arm. I was so perplexed, I turned in the opposite direction pulling Paul with me, it was the last thing I wanted for him to meet Dad.

Paul had already bought a double fronted semi-detached house, it looked so romantic. The house was built on a very steep slope with eighteen steps up to it. We now had to take a lot of time to buy the furniture, no expense was spared. I had no experience in these matters and would certainly have picked the most garish soft furnishings available. I am afraid Paul had to do all the choosing.

As the days went by I started to feel apprehensive. It was almost as if I was going along with it all, but not fully understanding what I was doing. One day I got so frustrated with it all, that I put on my jeans and went climbing in the small park at the side of the convent. Another day I went along to Sheila's house to listen to the latest pop records. I really was still very immature. One morning I got out of bed to find that I was bleeding. I knew what it was, but didn't know how to deal with it. This seems improbable given the many debauched women that I had associated with, however, they would happily discuss their sex lives, but had never touched on this topic. I was seventeen and it was my first period. What a dilemma. I felt that I could not speak to Sister Maria about it, perhaps nuns didn't have periods, what with them being so holy. It was impossible to go to work until the matter was resolved but I just didn't know what to do. With a flash of inspiration, I rushed out to the telephone box on the corner and rang Miss Stewart. "Now what's the problem Pearl?" she asked, wearily, on hearing the panic in my voice. After I explained my situation I could hear the sigh of relief in her voice, it was obvious that she had thought that I was in trouble yet again. "Go back to the convent, I'll be with you in half an hour."

She came prepared with the necessary items, explaining what to do. It had never occurred to anyone that I hadn't matured. Miss Stewart observed, "Well at least you have become a woman before your wedding day." She then gave me a lift into work and explained my little problem to Molly, my manager.

Molly was a married woman, childless by choice, she was a larger than life character, and possessed a terrific sense of humour. Playfully, she called me 'Her Little Slob'. This did not worry me in the least, I had been called far worse. Molly could not comprehend my little predicament of that morning.

There were now three weeks to go to my wedding day. I laid in bed at night listening to the nuns chant at the altar, the melodious sound was almost hypnotic. It made me feel at peace with myself, which in turn made me think more deeply, a luxury that I had never indulged in. In the past, thinking had always been a too painful experience. Most of my life I had lived for the moment, the future had never seemed very exciting, but now I was getting worried. Marriage was long term, was it what I really wanted? Paul was a kind, gentle person, I thought a lot of him, but did I love him, or was I simply escaping? Had the powers that be, purely given me permission to marry in order to discharge their responsibility of me? What about the physical side of marriage, would I be okay?

There were so many questions unanswered, I needed to get an unbiased opinion, but from whom? All of my mates were single, sixteen and seventeen year olds, everyone else was in some way involved in my past life. This was the time when I felt really alone in the world, when a mother or mother substitute would have come in handy. The previous few weeks of bustle, what with the house and wedding preparations, had been exciting. I had been caught up in the moment, now I desperately needed help to sort out my brain.

Everything became burdensome, even work became a drag. One day Molly said to me, "For goodness sake lift your face off the floor, you are depressing me, you should be happy, you are getting married in two weeks time." All my doubts came pouring out. Laughing, she explained that all brides had these doubts, it was just prenuptial nerves, she was also highly amused that I was so inexperienced. By the end of the day I felt a lot better and began to look forward to the big day.

The replies to the wedding invitations had all been received, one hundred guests were to attend. My side consisted mainly of children's officers, house mothers and probation officers. The only four family guests I had invited were, Uncle Charles and Auntie Nellie, Grandpa and my brother Peter, who I had managed to recently locate, much to my delight. I had not chosen any of them to give me away. I had forgiven my uncle and grandpa for not taking me in, but not enough to make either of them a major principal in my big day. My guest of honour was to be Mary Stewart, she had been the only adult person, other than the doctor at St. Cuthberts, who had ever tried to understand me and try to put me on any sort of right road.

Three days before the wedding, I picked my wedding attire up from the bridal shop. Taking it back to the convent, I hung the gown on the outside of the wardrobe door, this seemed to disturb Sister Maria, bitterly, she told me to put the dress out of sight. She did not feel at ease with me until the wedding morning, when she apologised to me for being off-hand, it was possibly a case of unrequited love, I'll never know.

The big day arrived and the nuns rallied around to help my bridesmaids and myself to get ready. The nuns were now very excited, it was not every day that a marriage procession left from the convent. They explained that they could not attend the Nuptial Mass in the main nave of the Church, but they would stand at the back behind the iron gates near to the font.

The wedding car arrived along with Jim Liquorish, Paul's business partner. Jim was to give me away. It was a freezing cold day, being mid December, I shivered as I stood by the door of the small church of St. Peter. I was not sure whether it was with cold or apprehension.

Resplendent in white gown, with veil covering my face, the walk down the aisle began. My eyes filled with tears, not tears of sadness but of happiness. I took my place beside my husband-to-be, and lifted my eyes to the altar. I thanked God that my childhood had gone, I was now nobodies property, I was my own person and could now live my life as I felt fit.

The Children's Committee could now close down their files on me, tie them with green ribbon and archive them. I dearly hoped that I could do the same with my childhood.

CHAPTER TWENTY FIVE

The reception over, Paul and I set off on our honeymoon to London, travelling in his small Bond Mini car. I was very excited when we arrived at our venue 'The Cora Hotel'. This was the first time that I was to be a paying guest in a hotel. The surroundings seemed very lavish to me, crystal chandeliers adorned the ceiling and the pile in the carpets almost swallowed me up. The hotel porter appeared in the reception to show us to our room, this made me feel very posh and important and much to Paul's amusement I began to flaunt airs and graces far beyond my normal station in life, lavishly tipping the porter with a crisp pound note. The bedroom was large and spacious having the added bonus of a en-suite bathroom, a luxury beyond compare for normal working class people in the fifties. It was usually queue up in the corridor on a first come, first served basis.

Champagne, chocolates and a vase of red roses were arranged on a polished table; everything was so splendid and romantic. I felt as though I was a film star about to star in her first romantic movie. This surely was the life I could get used to. After freshening up my husband and I went down to the dining room for the evening meal, which was served from silver salvers by a waiter in a dinner suit. I felt like the bee's knees and chicken eyebrows all rolled into one. To say I was mesmerised would have been an understatement. After dinner it was off around London for a sightseeing tour, which to me was truly magical, being mid-December the city was sparkling with the grandeur of the Christmas decorations, trees and fairy lights. Paul knew London well, he was a good guide, showing me the most splendid places, far more than I had seen when I had ran away from Leicester to London a couple of years earlier.

All too soon it was time to return to the hotel and get down to the more serious side of the honeymoon, the very thought of what was to come made my stomach perform somersaults. Once inside our room a terrible shyness took over me, I could have turned and run. Paul cracked open the champagne; forcing the cork to fly across the room, which left me giggling uncontrollably. Soon the sparkling liquid made me feel light-headed and a little calmer. "Time for bed now Pearl," Paul said in a matter of a fact way and disappeared into the bathroom to prepare himself. Not at all like the cinema I remember thinking. Half and hour passed and Paul emerged smelling like a flower garden adorned in blue silk pyjamas. I looked at him shyly and dashed into the bathroom, bolting the door firmly behind me. I could hardly breathe, my heart was pounding ten to the dozen, I was so scared. I know the post nuptials were about to begin. I could hear the priest's voice in my head, "With my body I thee honour," and the full meaning of the vows became obvious. Stripping off my clothes I looked into the full-length mirror at the back of the bath and studied my reflection. A slim almost boyish figure with very small breasts mirrored back at me, this did nothing at all to inspire me. What would Paul think when he saw me like this in the nuddy? I had always padded my bra out with ankle socks to give me a better shape, and now the truth would out. He wouldn't think much of this figure that stared back at me, I shouldn't think. I shuddered perishing the thought, where was all this sex appeal I supposedly oozed, it had seemed to have got up and abandoned me. I slipped into a hot foaming bath allowing the bubbles to envelop me and lay there for what seemed an age. Paul soon became impatient awaiting his conjugal rights, because he yelled through the bathroom door enquiring if I intended to stay in the bath all night.

After almost half an hour I emerged in my skimpy night dress, dashed across the bedroom floor, flew into the bed and covered myself quickly with the covers, my heart still beating ten to the dozen. Paul was bemused by the whole episode and calmly bid me a good night, by just pecking me on lightly the cheek. Phew, I though to myself as I began to relax, I've got away with the business tonight. But I was sadly mistaken.

During the ensuing lovemaking I became completely rigid, it was almost as if every bone in my body would snap. I just couldn't understand why my friends had raved so much about this sexual act. Thoughts of Jean and her defilement of my body, and my Christmas Dad all came rushing back to haunt me. I felt very dirty and must have been a grave disappointment to my new husband.

Things did improve a little over the next few days, but unfortunately we were forced to cut the honeymoon short and head for home, due to me contacting severe cystitis. Once home I settled into the routine of being a housewife, an appalling one at that, all the years of cooking and cleaning in the children's homes had not paid off. My idea of a thorough clean was a quick hoover and a lick and a promise with a duster or dishcloth, surface clean that was me.

It soon became evident that I was pregnant and began to suffer very badly, my health began to deteriorate. Eventually after six months the baby died inside of me, forcing me to have an operation to remove the child. I was not only upset but very, very angry. Once again something that I dearly wanted had been at hands reach and then taken from me at the final snatch. After I was fully recovered I went on a wild spree. Paul had gifted me with a '*Vespa*' motor scooter. I would pick up my friend Sheila Fritche and travel for miles, allowing the wind to blow in my hair, crash helmets were not obligatory in those days. I would frequent dance halls and pubs without Paul, often coming home the worse for wear, after downing numerous 'Barley Wines'.

Paul had not wanted intercourse since the loss of the baby, that side of our marriage was dead. Although I now had emotions and feelings which were often difficult to ignore. If I brought the subject up with him he changed the conversation rapidly. His mother had died whilst giving birth to him and he felt that he was going to destroy me in the same manner.

Paul put up with my wild behaviour for almost a year then one day in a fit of temper he told me, "Enough is enough, either you settle down and be a good wife or I shall ask you to leave." His words shook me rigid, after many tears and sulks I thought I had better give the marriage my best shot. After all, I had been acting like a single badly behaved teenager. At eighteen it was time I grew up and faced my responsibilities, because I was very silly and immature and Paul had been more than patient with me. Not once had I taken into account his feelings at the loss of our child. This made me realise how selfish I had been.

I began to buckle down and clean the house in a respectable way, finding skirting boards and the like that I had never knew existed. Then my mind once again turned to becoming a mother. However Paul was still ignoring the sexual side of our marriage, it never occurred to him that he wasn't being a proper husband. But he was gentle and kind in many other ways, he lavished me with gifts, but what I really wanted was what I never had, affection and deep undivided love. We had now become more like brother and sister, not a very good basis for a marriage.

My friends were now beginning to get married and soon some were pregnant. My envy became so deep it was almost phobic. I so wanted a baby of my own to love and cuddle.

One day in desperation I called into the Catholic church of 'St. Peter's where I had been married. I knelt before 'The Lady Altar' and prayed like I had never prayed before.

Surely this time, God just for once would answer my prayer, I was only asking for the most natural thing on earth, motherhood. I had never been a very devout Christian, what one would call luke warm really. However I thought I would give it a go, after all other folks seem to have their prayers answered.

Suddenly as I knelt there, 'The Virgin Mary' appeared to walk towards me with a smile on her face and her hands held in the air. I was petrified and ran from the church as fast as my legs could carry me. I did not think for one minute that it was a figment of my imagination. With the exception of Sheila I dared not tell anyone, I certainly didn't want any one to think I had lost my marbles or worse. Even more amazing, without any provocation Paul began to perform that night. I became pregnant and nine months later gave birth to my first son Andrew Phillip. Fact being stranger than fiction he was born as clean as a silver whistle, with just a cross of red blood on his forehead. He was a wonderful ten pound baby with blond curly hair. Paul was so proud of his son and lavished all his spare time and affection on him, which of cause again left me out in the cold.

I believe I was a good mother and spent many hours playing and talking to my son. His clothes were the best that money could buy. There was every toy imaginable in his nursery, even royalty would have been envious. No money or love was spared on that little boy.

When Andrew was four months old his weight began to fall, after many tests it was found that he had been born with a lack of calcium, soon he was having surgery on his legs and joints to correct them. Most of my time was spent at the hospital, feeding and caring for him. I found it a huge struggle nursing a sick child, but I knew I must do it.

Once home from the hospital life became tiring, Andrew had both of his legs in plaster of Paris and he found it very difficult to sleep. The responsibility was overwhelming to me.

My marriage was failing fast now, Paul was not showing me any affection at all, I was at a low ebb and wept buckets of tears during this time, always exploring in my mind what my next move should be. It seemed to me that I was a failure at every thing I did. For a time and out of character I really wallowed in self-pity.

Andrew became stronger and began to walk, but I was always restless, I would tie him to my waist and travel around with him on the back of my scooter. We moved house four times in as many years, each time I felt that I had found my dream home only to become bored and disillusioned within months.

Paul was now at his wits end, he still wanted me as his companion but not as his lover. He suggested that we go and live overseas, first it was India for a year, travelling to Singapore and then it was New Zealand. Two new continents could not repair our marriage so it was back to England. We bought a lovely house in a beautiful village named Kirby Muxloe in Leicestershire and we tried to settle down. It proved too difficult, we both led separate lives even having separate bedrooms. I found myself a job and realised I could be independent. I also started to study at the local Polytech.

I had now become a woman with all of a woman's longings and my marriage was a sham, it was being held together for the united love of our son. The priest Father Rousseau spent more time at our house counselling us than he did at the church. He eventually formed the opinion that our marriage could not be saved.

I moved out of the marital home into an attic flat, leaving Andrew with his father during the week and taking custody of him at the weekends. I was very lonely and soon turned my attentions to finding another partner. After some time I met my present husband Bryon who could offer me all the things I had been looking for and before long I had moved in with him and his son Martyn, which was to prove to be a bad move at the time. By the time my divorce came to court I was well into pregnancy by Bryon with my second son Bryon his father's namesake. At the divorce hearing which was a long drawn out affair, the judge concluded that I was living in immoral surroundings and I lost complete custody of my son. Cohabiting was really frowned upon in the Sixties, it was either called living over the brush or living in sin, which I always interpreted as being an abbreviation of sincerity. The loss of my son tore me apart for quite some time to come, I do not know what I would have done without the support and strength of Bryon.

The arrangement that Paul and I had before had always worked admirably. The fact that I had been in a mental institution in my early teens had also gone against me, in my cross petition custody case. Bryon was also awarded the cost and a fine for causing the breakdown of the marriage, which was completely perverse. It caused us great hardship having to find money on a monthly basis.

My childhood immaturity and lack of worldly knowledge almost certainly was the beginning of the end for my marriage to Paul, it had doom written all over it from the very beginning. I had been so intent in locking away my past that my present had intertwined.

Once my second child had been born I decided to take a full stock take of my life, I wrote off the useless things and retained my assets, which could be profitable to my future. If I had allowed myself to continue along the same road, the people who had stolen my childhood, would have stolen the rest of my life. I just could not let that happen.

With the help of Bryon's love and friendship I knew I had accomplished my aim when I became a Director of a medium sized company. It was at this stage that I knew I was on a winning streak at last.

My journey through the past has proved to be a very painful one. My hope that whoever reads this book will reflect on the great gift which they have been given by the birth of their children. They are not only your present but also your future, representatives of yourselves. Yours for a short time to love and guide until they become their own people manifesting all the good things, which hopefully you will have taught them.

Forget the words of the old adage spare the rod

and spoil the child, it is a load of rubbish. Take it from one who knows. Physical pain heals, the scars show, but become painless. Mental ones are deeply ingrained and the unseen scars are forever painful, rearing their heads at the most inopportune times.

As for my feelings towards my Mother Eva, I conclude that they are borne out of pity and not love. It would be foolish of me to convince my readers otherwise. Eva had a painful and pitiful life, she was not to blame for my lost childhood.

Some months before Eva died, whilst we were chatting about my childhood, she gave me the only bit of advice that she had ever proffered. Her words were, "We all have a set of circumstances, which we must live by. I learned to live within mine, please try and live within yours Pearl." Let's hope that all of your children's circumstances are excellent.